The LORD is good to those whose hope is in ......,
to the one who seeks him.

Lamentations 3:25

May you come to find the Lord within
the pages of this book.

GOD ALLOWS U-TURNS
A Woman's Journey

True Stories of Hope
and Healing

ALLISON GAPPA BOTTKE
with Cheryll Hutchings

PROMISE PRESS
An Imprint of Barbour Publishing

GOD ALLOWS U-TURNS

A Woman's Journey

Through Jesus, therefore, let us continually offer to God a sacrifice of praise—the fruit of lips that confess his name. And do not forget to do good and to share with others, for with such sacrifices God is pleased.

Hebrews 13:15–16

FOR OUR CONTRIBUTORS AND READERS

As always, this book is dedicated to our brothers and sisters in Christ who sent us stories, and to our readers around the world who will come to depend upon this and future volumes of *God Allows U-Turns* to uplift and encourage them in their personal walk of faith. It is our prayer that God will be pleased with the fruit of sharing offered by the contributors whose true stories appear in this third volume of *God Allows U-Turns*.

May these slice-of-life stories touch your emotions and warm your heart. May they bring you to a better understanding of God's love for us all.

God's peace and protection to you always.

ALLISON

In Honor of
Connor John Endriss
God loves you, and so does your grandma.

In Prayer for
Gene, Carol, J.P., and April
May God continue to give you strength.

In Memory of
Kassandra Lee Gazda
Rest in peace, little one, as your heavenly Father holds your hand.

CONTENTS

SIXTEEN—THANKFULNESS

FOREWORD

"What the world needs now is love, sweet Love. It's the only thing that there's just too little of." Remember the song? I sure do. While those words rang forth from radios years ago, today they speak loudly from the voices of hurting women everywhere. We need love, and it's not that there is too little of it to go around; it's that many of us don't know where to find it.

And so we look for love in all the wrong places. We seek out platonic and sexual relationships, try to build financial nest eggs, shop until we drop, and affiliate with one group and then another. We eat and drink our way to an early grave, gambling and partying with little reservation, and chase a myriad of religions. We throw ourselves into trying to change others so we don't have to look at the mess we have made of our own lives. Extreme behaviors abound; you name it and women everywhere are doing it, searching for a fantasy love that simply does not exist.

Over the past twenty-two years I have taught, counseled, mentored, and lectured to millions of women and, through it all, I have discovered a frightening truth. Women everywhere are seeking, searching, needing, and longing for self-acceptance and the acceptance of someone or something to validate us with love—no matter what. It's the "no matter what" situations that leave many of us in compromising—even life-threatening—situations only because we need someone with skin on him or her to make us feel loved. These "no matter what situations" have steered women down a narrow, two-lane highway on the wrong side of the road. Women everywhere are heading the wrong direction, on a collision course waiting to crash.

What's surprising is that many of us know we are

going the wrong way—yet we feel powerless to stop. It's like driving on a mountain road and not seeing anyplace to turn around. Sometimes on this highway, boulders from the mountains are on the road—stopping us dead in our tracks. Sometimes the fog is so heavy and the mist is so deep that we can't see the road directly in front of our eyes. Yet we keep driving, hoping for a way out—praying for the ability to turn around.

And praise God we can turn around because *God Allows U-Turns!* No matter how far off course we have gone, there is a place designated for a safe U-turn. There is even Someone at that place who will go along with us on the journey—Someone who will offer us safety, comfort, strength, peace, contentment, hope, grace, faithfulness, kindness, gentleness, patience, and even a level of control. This person's name is *Love.* This person's name is *Jesus.*

Women, rejoice with me! We no longer have to stay on the highway of despair. We can learn from our sisters who have traveled the rocky roads and come out on the other side with wisdom and courage. *A Woman's Journey* leads us over the mountains and through the hills, down into the pits and up to the pinnacle, through success and failure, hurt and heroism, wandering and wonderment, pitiful to powerful road trips. In every journey in these true stories, women have ultimately found Love in the right places, smack-dab in the middle of their circumstances. Sometimes Love was standing back waiting for them to acknowledge Him. Come with me on an exhilarating woman's journey. Glimpse into the lives of these triumphant women as they seek direction from a Navigator who helps get them back on track. Each of us will be able to find a shared truth in one or more of these stories of hope and healing. "What the world needs now is love, sweet Love. It's the only thing that there's just too little of."

The heroic women in the following stories have found a safe place to make a successful U-turn on their journey from devastation to inspiration, directly into the arms of Love. Let them lead you to that place of refuge and safety. Let them lead you into the arms of Jesus.

> THELMA WELLS, Speaker/Author,
> President of A Woman of God Ministries
> and Mother of Zion Ministries
> Speaker for the Women of Faith Conferences,
> Dallas, Texas

Introduction

Dear Reader:

While reading the thousands of stories submitted for this volume, *A Woman's Journey,* I realized that women walk many of the same paths in life. As daughters, sisters, friends, wives, mothers, and grandmothers, we all share the sometimes painful consequences of taking wrong directions. We have all, at one time or another, gone down the wrong path, whether in thought, action, or deed.

My heart broke as I read stories of abuse, addiction, abortion, divorce, rape, incest, death, shame, guilt, and fear. But I also rejoiced with thanksgiving as contributors shared how faith in God brought hope and healing. Oh, my dear sisters in Christ! How my arms long to wrap around each of you in a sisterly embrace. Being able to share these intimate moments has made me stronger—and will help make many others stronger—as we see God at work.

Many of us will relate to one or more of the provocatively honest stories in this volume. We do not sugarcoat the difficult journeys our writers have shared. In fact, the candidness of topics in *God Allows U-Turns* boldly goes where many short-story anthologies fear to tread.

These profound experiences make us the women we are. Being able to confront my own painful past has been liberating. I used to believe people who prayed were weak—that believing in God was an old-fashioned tradition reserved for senior citizens and little children, or for people who "didn't know any better." I was above all that "religious nonsense." I charted my own course, believing only in myself, and that I was the "master of my destiny." Aided by New Age philosophies, astrological charts, an occasional tarot card reading, and a secular worldview that "god is within me," I was adrift on a sea of confusion, void of any truthful direction.

Now, those years seem like a lifetime ago. If you have read the introductions to volumes one and two in the U-Turns series, you know all about my life-changing U-turn toward God. You know that in 1989 I found peace and direction, that I filled that empty place in my heart and soul with a relationship—not a religion. A relationship with Jesus Christ. Second Corinthians 5:17 touched my soul and became real to me: "Therefore, if anyone is in Christ, he is a new creation; the old has gone, the new has come!" I was "new," and as I grew in the Lord, so did my desire to spread the Word.

Many women today live just as I did. . .lost and alone . . .yet going through the motions of "getting by." Many of us have been discouraged over the years. Many of us have faced setback after setback, wondering if things will ever work out in our favor. . .if the trials and tribulations will ever stop. We desperately need hope and healing.

When Jesus walked the earth as a man, He taught mostly by sharing stories, or "parables." Jesus understood the power of a story—especially true stories as they related to His teachings.

True human-interest stories touch us in ways we can't always explain, affecting all of us differently. We often gain wisdom from a story that speaks to our heart. That is what *God Allows U-Turns* is all about: speaking to our hearts.

God is encouraging His children to step out in faith as never before, to challenge the false values that seem to be taking over our world. The stories in this book are about faith and how vital it is to be a believer every minute of every day. . .not just for an hour on Sunday or at Christmas and Easter. A revival of believers is stepping forward to be counted—no matter the cost. Believers ready to share their quiet faith, bold faith, wavering faith, fallen faith, and resurrected faith. Not so long ago I scoffed at believers such as these. Today I call them my most treasured and beloved family.

Dear reader, I pray that no matter where you are in your walk of faith, you will let the messages of these stories touch your heart and soul; that you will read these little slice-of-life messages as parables for our time.

I also pray that if the Lord draws you closer to Him, you will turn to the page at the back of this book that tells how to experience a U-turn in your life. If you know someone else who needs the hope and healing only our Lord Jesus Christ can bring, share that page—and this book—with your hurting friend or loved one.

Speaking of "pages at the back of the book," please take a few minutes to read about the awesome outreach of the God Allows U-Turns Project. Our foundation is donating a percentage of proceeds from this book to several nonprofit faith-based organizations. You can also read about future volumes and how you can send us your true short story for consideration in a future volume.

Volume four in the series will be a special treasure, tentatively titled: *God Allows U-Turns—American Moments: True Stories of Hope and Healing from Times of National Crisis*. This poignant volume will share courageous stories of how God has made Himself real to Americans. How our faith has increased as we have weathered the storms of such national moments as the Great Depression, world wars, Pearl Harbor, the Oklahoma City bombing, the Columbine High School shooting, airline disasters, natural disasters, and, of course, the tragic events of September 11, 2001. You won't want to miss this volume!

You can keep up-to-date on the God Allows U-Turns Project by frequently visiting our web site at www.-godallowsuturns.com.

In closing, the authors and contributors whose stories appear here have opened their hearts and souls to us. They are warriors proclaiming their faith. Thank you for spending time with them. Thank you for sharing this book with other family and friends. And, remember, we are all family—and that bond, combined with God's promises and direction for our lives, is our saving grace. Never forget that our God is a God of second chances and new beginnings. And never, ever forget that our *God Allows U-Turns!*

May God's peace, protection, and direction be with you always.

Your Sister in Christ,
ALLISON
editor@godallowsuturns.com
www.godallowsuturns.com

Chapter
One

New Direction U-Turns

Therefore, if anyone is in Christ, he is a new creation;
the old has gone, the new has come!

2 Corinthians 5:17

Bull's-Eye

by Allison Gappa Bottke
Faribault, Minnesota

"Allison, call me on my cell phone when you get in. It's important," was the message I retrieved from my hotel voice mail at 7:30 P.M. on October 3, 1998. While my stepson's voice was calm, I knew in my heart something terrible had happened. My mind raced as I returned his call, imagining all sorts of life-and-death scenarios, knowing for certain whatever had happened involved my husband of only three years.

"Dad's been in an accident. Aaron sort of got him," came Kermit's reply to my "what's wrong" question. "Aaron?" It took a minute for my mind to compute that he was referring to our fifteen-hundred-pound Hereford herd bull. "Define 'sort of got him,' " I cried. "Is he dead?" Cutting right to the chase is my nature; I had to know the truth.

"No," came his tentative reply. "But they're taking him into surgery right now. He's beat up pretty bad. He might lose his leg. He wasn't gored as far as they can see, but it's too soon to tell. Can you come home?"

Thus began my trek from Ohio to Minnesota via car as I couldn't get a flight until the next morning, and time was too precious to wait.

"Dear God," I cried out, "please keep Kevin safe; please be with the doctors and give them wisdom to make the right choices," I prayed as I frantically drove home. "Please spare my husband. I can't lose him now, not when we've only just begun our life together."

Kevin had been working on our farm that day, building a corral with Kermit, his oldest son, and Matt, our hired hand. They had put in a rather long day when Kermit was finishing up on the skid loader, Matt was moving hay bales on the tractor, and Kevin was in the farmyard working around the cows. Having grown up on a farm, Kevin had always exhibited a healthy respect for our bull, teaching me never to turn my back on him. That day—and it's hard to say why it happened—Aaron suddenly and without warning came after Kevin, and with the powerful butt of his head, sent my husband flying into the air. In no time he had Kevin back on the ground, rolling him, stepping on him, and pounding him into the dirt.

Hearing nothing over the sounds of the tractor and the skid loader, it was by the grace of God that Matt looked up just as Kevin was flying through the air, and he frantically began waving to Kermit, who was closer to the situation.

"I looked up and saw Aaron on top of Dad, bashing him into the concrete base of the corn silo," Kermit said, fighting back tears as he explained to me what happened. "He kept butting him with his head. Dad was rolled up in a ball and I thought for sure he was dead." Thinking quickly, Kermit remained on the skid loader and as fast as he could, he drove straight into the side of the raging bull, knocking him off his feet and away from Kermit's now-silent father. That act alone saved Kevin's life.

"By the time the bull had me down the second time, I knew I was a dead man," said Kevin. "I can clearly remember being thankful that I knew Jesus as my Lord and Savior. I was prepared to go to heaven."

"By the time I got to Dad, he was pretty beat up, but I thanked God when I could see that he was still alive," Kermit said. "But he was covered in blood, and his left leg was at an impossible angle. I knew it was broken. I couldn't tell if Aaron's massive horns had punctured him. My immediate concern was to keep the bull away from him and try to keep Dad as quiet as possible until the ambulance could arrive."

"Most bull attacks are fatal, and I figured this would be such a case," admitted Mike David, a paramedic and Kevin's longtime acquaintance. "When we got the call, my heart jumped to my throat, knowing Kevin as I did."

But the Lord did not call Kevin home. Instead He sent us both on a journey of hope and healing that changed our lives.

Kevin was rushed to the Mayo Clinic with a pulverized tibia, fractured fibula, facial lacerations, and head-to-toe bruises. The surgical team was soon faced with a severe "compartment syndrome" in his leg as they prepared to operate—a syndrome that causes intense swelling, often resulting in the need to amputate limbs as a result of dead muscle, tissue, and nerves.

"I had never seen an injury quite like it," said Dr. Brian Hamline, the attending orthopedic surgeon on call that night. "In any other hospital, especially in a small town, his leg most likely would have been amputated, but at Mayo we had a team of highly skilled surgeons, all focused on doing whatever it took to save that leg." And save it they did.

Thus began the yearlong siege of my sweet husband, a man whose last stay in the hospital had been when he entered the world in 1954.

After three weeks and five surgeries, including multiple bone and skin grafts, Kevin left St. Mary's Mayo Medical Center wearing an external "fixator"—a bizarre-looking contraption that consisted of three metal halos and twelve pins going through his bones from his ankle to his knee. He would wear this equipment for twelve long months, unable to bear any weight whatsoever on that leg for nine of those months. A walker, then crutches, assisted him for one full year.

Through it all, I witnessed the perseverance of an optimist whose eyes were on the Lord. Seldom did he cry out when I know the pain was intolerable. He was a most gracious patient, and I reveled in the ability to care for him as my nurturing nature took over, trying to make my husband's recuperation and rehabilitation as comfortable as humanly possible. I hovered over him like a protective lioness—vowing nothing further would harm him while he healed.

I frequently cried out to God, asking for His will to be done, asking for guidance when my nerves were frayed, and thanking Him for the ability to stay at home full time to care for Kevin

This was a time of great change in our lives. Kevin temporarily turned over the reins of his hugely successful real estate business to a coworker, and I began to write again, something I had put on the back burner when we married in 1995. A previously planned winter vacation was rescheduled for the next year, giving Kevin a goal to work toward as he vowed to "leave these stupid crutches behind" as we ushered in the new millennium on the beach at South Padre Island, Texas.

It was on that beach in Texas fourteen months after the accident that we praised the Lord for saving Kevin's life and his leg. We held hands as he walked with the aid of only a cane, sharing our dreams and visions for our future. Kevin would start his own real estate company and venture out on his own, away from the constraints of corporate America. I would dust off the *God Allows U-Turns* manuscript and, after some major revisions, begin once again to look for a publisher.

"It seems everyone has a story to tell," I shared with Kevin as we walked on the beach. The year we spent in and out of the hospital, doctors' offices, and in physical therapy brought us countless stories from folks whose lives had been spared by God's amazing grace. We were often in awe at how open people were in sharing their deeply personal stories of hope and healing. "Perhaps God doesn't want my own U-turn story to be published because this is bigger than just my story," I told Kevin. "Maybe I could make this a compilation. I wonder if people would send me their stories of faith if I asked?"

The rest, as they say, is history.

From out of the ashes of pain came Kevin's vision to operate a real estate company whose foundation is Christ, and today his company is making history in our town as one of the fastest-growing, most ethical businesses around. And as for me? Well, my passion to share the hope and healing of turning toward Christ has become a growing outreach ministry through the God Allows U-Turns Project. Thousands of stories come to me through my Web site each month. The Lord brought me an amazing Web site designer, a world-class literary agent, an international publisher, and an eager team of co-editors and publicity and promotions volunteers. Even more important is the Lord's gift of a growing audience of readers whose thirst to read U-turn stories is growing with each and every volume published.

It took a life-threatening accident to make us

reassess our lives. To help us turn our hearts and minds toward the God who held us up when we were too weak to walk. And just think, it really was a bull that helped us hit the bull's-eye in knowing and following God's will for our lives. Imagine that.

A Whirlwind Way of Life

by Nancy B. Gibbs
Cordele, Georgia

I looked back and wondered how it all began. The craziness didn't start overnight, but gradually became a reality. I wondered how to get out of the whirlwind but didn't have a clue. The push to achieve and the vision of success filled my mind and kept me going.

"If only I made a little more money," I decided one day after struggling with the monthly bills. At the time I had a part-time job an hour away from home. Since my husband was a pastor, I held many responsibilities in our church. That occupied my Sundays and Wednesday nights. I then found another part-time job, which took up the four days a week that I wasn't working at the other job. Before long, I added even another job to my list of things to do.

With three jobs, one teenage child at home and two in college, the duties associated with being a pastor's wife, and a house to keep, I was exhausted. In addition, I continued to struggle to pay the bills. The extra expenses associated with work were enormous. The gasoline, the take-out meals, taxes, extra work clothes, and the "I owe it to myself money" took most of my small paychecks. There was a small amount left to pay the bills, however, so I continuously struggled to earn more money, thinking that at some point in time, I could stop the insanity. I didn't think I could afford to give up even one job as long as college tuition and bills had to be paid.

I pushed myself to the limit. Physical ailments began to surface. "How am I going to pay these doctor and medication bills?" I wondered. But I kept pushing and achieving. I thought that one day all of this craziness would pay off. But it never did.

During this difficult period of time, my father became terminally ill. I spent a great deal of time sitting beside his bed and holding his hand. The nursing home was an hour away, so I should have limited my visits. Instead, I found myself on the interstate sometimes six times a week.

Nighttime visits became frequent. Many nights I drove home so sleepy that I felt like I couldn't see straight. But with three jobs and the other responsibilities, I thought I had to keep on trudging along at any expense.

One night, as I was driving home on the interstate, an anxiety attack got my attention. I couldn't breathe, swallow, or see well. I started perspiring profusely and felt as though I was going to get sick. The entire time, trucks and cars were whizzing by me, making my head spin. I stopped at a rest area briefly to catch my breath and then decided to try driving the last twenty miles. The entire way home, I prayed that God would get me there safely. I made many promises to Him during that trip.

"If You'll get me home safely tonight, Lord, I'll slow down," I whispered. "I'll give up some of these overwhelming responsibilities, drive this distance less often, and serve You more." I drove at a snail's pace in the right lane of the interstate the remainder of the way home. Even though trucks and cars continued to fly by me, I made it home safely. My husband and daughter met me at the car. When I stepped out, I became very sick. The entire next day, I stayed in bed and cried a river of tears. I prayed diligently, asking God to help me escape the whirlwind.

Gradually, I changed my lifestyle just as I had promised God. That night on the interstate was a U-turn in my life. God literally changed my direction. Over the next few years, I eliminated two jobs and ended up with one part-time job that I dearly love. I continued to visit Dad two days a week until he left this world almost a year ago. My house is clean and comfortable. My family is happy, and I have begun to heal.

Today, I miss my father, and sometimes my home gets lonely since my grown children have moved away. I continue to enjoy my part-time job, but I also take pleasure in full-time living. I had put my life on hold for so long that it took some adjustment to slow down and enjoy simple pleasures again. But with God's help, I became successful at that, too.

Currently, I spend my spare time writing about things that are important to me. Expressing my feelings on paper has a way of healing my soul. Our finances are now in order. Our tithes far exceed the amount we were able to give during the time I was caught in a whirlwind.

I thought the dependence on jobs, money, and things would eventually pay off and make me happy. But I discovered that real success came the day I stopped depending on the world and turned my eyes toward Jesus. Placing my faith in Him made all the difference. I'm so thankful He saw me home that horrible night and that He washed my eyes with tears so I could finally see again.

One Small Loaf of Bread

by Kris Decker
Blaine, Minnesota

"Man does not live on bread alone" (Luke 4:4). It was a verse I'd heard all my life. But eleven years ago I learned a person could live quite well on bread, especially when it comes from a divine source.

I was only thirty years old at the time, living in the rubble of what had once been my carefully constructed life. My six-year marriage had crumbled, I was raising my daughter alone, and I was working two jobs to support our little household. Anxiety and fear settled over me like a cloud of ashes as my bank balance dwindled and my debts mounted. Just when I thought things could not disintegrate any further, my ex-husband stopped paying child support. No matter how many hours I worked, I couldn't earn enough to make ends meet without that monthly check.

Although I was on my own financially, I received emotional support from my new friends—people I'd recently met in a twelve-step group, along with my neighbors, all of whom just happened to be Christians. They told me if I turned my life over to the care of my loving Father in heaven, He would help me. I had to admit it sounded good. But like those ads I'd seen posted on power-line poles—"Lose 30 pounds in 30 days"—it seemed too good to be true.

I moved forward cautiously. Unlike others who describe the beginning of their spiritual journey as a leap of faith, mine was more like tiptoeing toward trust. Warily, I accepted my neighbor's invitation to attend her church.

"Just one time," I told her, fearing entrapment, brainwashing, or some other kind of manipulation lying in wait.

"Of course," she said. "No pressure."

Much to my surprise, it was a pleasant experience. The people were kind, and the doctrine made sense. Everything should have clicked right into place, but it didn't. My heart was shut tight, double-bolted with the security alarm fully activated. I was afraid. What if I did turn my life over to God and declare Jesus as my Savior? Did He really care about what happened to me? And who was I to even ask for help anyway?

Then a small loaf of bread arrived.

"At long last, the famine has ended! Look what I got today," I announced to my friends, dropping the freshly baked bread onto the table with a thud. They all stared, confused by the roll of my eyes and the sarcastic tone in my voice. "I got it from that church I've gone to a couple of times," I explained. "You know, the one my neighbor invited me to? They give this to all the new attendees." I laughed scornfully. "If this is God's way of feeding us, we're going to starve within a week."

It was like the worst kind of cruel joke. Only the day before, my mailbox had bulged with bills, each demanding immediate payment. The mortgage company, the electric company, and the city water co-op all tossed out threats like hand grenades: foreclosure, disconnection, discontinued service. Worse still, I didn't know where I was going to get money for food. Our refrigerator and cupboards echoed from bareness, and I wouldn't get a paycheck for another ten days. That small loaf of bread seemed to mock my situation. I could lose everything, and if this was God, why was He sending me this one pathetic, puny loaf of bread?

My friend Beth reached across the table and patted my hand. "Maybe this is God's way of letting you know He's going to take care of you," she said kindly.

"Yeah, right," I muttered, slumping down into my chair like a petulant teenager. I had plenty of reasons to feel cynical about getting assistance from God.

It wasn't that I didn't believe in Him. If anything, I believed too well the lessons I'd learned as a child in our "religious" home, memorizing doctrine that taught me I had to earn the trip to heaven. All of my life I'd felt like a kid selling candy for a school fund-raiser, never quite producing enough good acts, and ultimately falling short of my quota and the grand prize: an all-expense paid trip to paradise. Even more discouraging was the belief that God didn't really know or care about me personally, or so I'd been told. He was just too busy with more important things, they'd said—like wars and floods and the Super Bowl.

"Well, if God doesn't care about me," I'd decided, "then I am certainly not going to care about Him." And I closed and locked the door to my heart. There was no way He could get in, because only I possessed the key.

Later that evening, after I'd taken my bread home and tucked my daughter into bed, I sat down to think. One of my friends had given me a *Bible Promise Book,* which lists biblical promises related specifically to issues we face every day. I began glancing through it.

I'll just see what God has to say about money, I thought.

The defiant part of me wanted to challenge this seem-ingly foolish belief, while another part hoped to find some kind of fiscal Charles-Schwab-type advice in those pages. Randomly I flipped open the book, not to "Money" as I'd intended but to a section on "Faith." The verses all but jumped out of the book and shouted in my face.

"Believe in the Lord Jesus, and you will be saved—you and your household" (Acts 16:31).

"I have come into the world as a light, so that no one who believes in me should stay in darkness" (John 12:46).

"Then Jesus declared, 'I am the bread of life. He who comes to me will never go hungry, and he who believes in me will never be thirsty' " (John 6:35).

I know God's voice is almost always a still, small one—a whisper, a breeze, the gentlest of nudges. But that night was different. Like Saul of Tarsus, I needed to be blinded by a magnificent flash of light in order to see the truth. And I was, for there before me, spelled out in black and white, were the answers to every one of my problems—the house payment, the electric bill, the water bill, and food. If God had taken out a full-page ad in the *New York Times,* His message could not have been more obvious. The very thought of it took my breath away. At long last, the door to my heart flew open and com-pletely off its hinges.

I sank to my knees, and for the first time in my life, I cried out to God for His help. For the first time in my life, I really believed God heard.

Two days later, I received a phone call from the pas-tor at the "Loaf of Bread" church. He said he wanted to meet me. We agreed he would come to my home the fol-lowing evening.

When he arrived, I barely managed to open the door before he began to speak. He was grinning and nearly danced his way into my living room.

"I received a very clear message from the Holy Spirit concerning you," he said, smiling. "Here."

He pushed a piece of paper into my hand. Confused and a bit frightened, I slowly unfolded the paper, half expecting one of those pink phone messages one gets at the office, "While You Were Out, the Holy Spirit Called." But it wasn't that at all. It was a check for $1,000—the exact amount of money I needed to pay all of my bills and buy food.

The pastor told me it wasn't a loan, and there were no strings attached. I didn't need to do anything at all to deserve or earn this money. It was a gift, just like God's love. Just like Jesus' sacrifice on the cross.

I don't remember much else about that night. I think I was in shock, dazzled at the thought that the Creator of the universe did in fact love and care about me. Me! How could Someone so divine love me?

Even after all this time, I am still amazed by God's grace. But what's most remarkable is that God's intercession didn't end with the delivery of that check. Two months after I received it, I lost my house to foreclosure, my car to the junk pile, and my jobs to cutbacks and layoffs.

Like any good Father, God wanted not only to care for me but also to teach and guide me. Once I truly believed I wasn't too insignificant for God to love, then I needed to build on my faith, lean on God instead of the world, and trust He would always take care of me, even in the worst of times.

And He did. Because even after I lost all my material possessions, I discovered my life didn't end. In fact, the more I lost, the richer I became. When I surrendered my life's journey to God, He set me gently upon a new path and blessed me abundantly. Within two years after receiving the loaf of bread, I married a man rooted in his faith and belief in God. God gave us a second beautiful child and provided me with one miraculous opportunity after another to complete my education and begin a new career. He presented me with a quality of life, happiness, and peace that could only come from a benevolent Father who, in His infinite wisdom, knew all along what was best for me. The kind of Father who could take one small loaf of bread and feed me with it for the rest of my life.

Miracle on Mercer Street

by Carol Genengels
Seabeck, Washington

It was a balmy summer day with sunshine and gentle breezes. Seagulls screamed and fluttered in the blue skies as our family boarded the ferry bound for Seattle. We joined several church friends aboard the vessel. Everyone was excited about going to Seattle Center's opera house to see "Miracle on Azusa Street." A cast from California was presenting the musical as an evangelical outreach.

After the ferry docked, our party walked to a waterfront restaurant. Most of us ordered seafood, but five-year-old Ryan wanted a hamburger and fries. He was too excited to eat more than a few bites.

After lunch, we headed for the monorail that would zoom us to Seattle Center. I grasped Ryan's hand as we trudged up steep hills. His other fist clutched a doggie bag holding the remains of his lunch. We heard a chorus of groans as we approached the monorail terminal. It was closed for repairs. While some opted for taxies, the rest of us decided to catch a city bus.

Our gang spread out as we boarded the crowded motor coach. Ann, Ryan, and I found seats near the front of the bus. Ryan stared at the bedraggled stranger sitting across the aisle from us. He hungrily eyed Ryan's doggie bag.

"Would you like a hamburger?" Ryan asked the man.

The stranger nodded and mumbled "thanks" as he reached for the bag. His smile revealed missing teeth. Ryan's blue eyes watched intently as the man wolfed down the burger and fries. He wiped his mouth on the back of his hand.

"What's your name, little boy?"

"Ryan. What's yours?"

"The name's George. Thanks for the burger."

"You're welcome," Ryan said.

George brushed stringy black hair away from his brown eyes. "Where are you all going on this fine day?"

Ryan told him we were on our way to see a play.

"Oh," he said before proudly announcing, "I'm an American Indian."

"Really!" I said, joining the conversation. "My friend, Ann, has Indian blood, too."

Ann engaged George in a discussion about their common roots. He gave his full attention, but most of his responses didn't make much sense.

We reached our destination, and our gang filed off the bus. My husband, Ted, caught up with Ryan and grasped his hand. George got off, too, and fell into step behind us. His disheveled clothes reeked of body odor and stale urine.

"So. . .you're going to a play?" George asked.

"Yes, we are," Ted said.

"How much does the play cost?"

"Nothing. It's free!" Ted responded.

"Can anyone go?" George inquired.

"Sure," Ted answered. "Would you like to come with us?"

George nodded. Ann and I exchanged glances as we joined the throngs of well-dressed people assembled in front of the posh opera house. Massive doors swung open and we filed in. The splendid lobby impressed many, especially our guest. George stuck close to Ted as we made our way through the crowd. We were ushered down thick carpeting to the front of the theater. Our group settled in the first three rows. George had an aisle seat by Ted. Ryan and I sat on the other side of Ted. Ann settled in front of us.

Since we were early, we had plenty of free time before the play began. Ted did his best to ignore the rank odor as he treated George like an old friend. George began confiding in Ted, educating him about life on the streets. He confessed that he had "a bit of a drinking habit." George said he'd once been trapped in a fire that left his body covered with scars. He rolled up his shirt-sleeves, revealing some of the disfiguring welts.

Ann turned around from time to time to offer breath mints. Ted thanked her as much as George did.

Before long the huge opera house was packed. We had the best seats in the house. The din of voices quieted as the orchestra began playing and the curtain opened. We were soon carried away to Azusa Street as talented singers and actors portrayed the story.

When it came time for the intermission, George left his seat abruptly. Ted went looking for him, but couldn't find him in the crowded lobby. We were disappointed to think that George would miss the ending.

Shortly before the lights dimmed, George returned to his seat. His hair was slicked back, and he had washed his face and hands. Somewhere beneath the grimy exterior lived the soul of a ruggedly handsome man. I overheard George confide in Ted, "You know, my mother has been praying for me for years and years, always begging God to save me. I guess I gave her a pretty hard time in the past."

The lights faded and the music began. As the story progressed toward the climax, George repeatedly brushed tears from his eyes. He wasn't the only one.

The play ended with an altar call. Young and old alike streamed toward the stage to dedicate their lives to the Lord. George was at the head of the line.

We bid our new brother in Christ good-bye as we exited the grand opera house. George held his head a little higher as he slowly made his way down Mercer Street and disappeared into the crowd.

My Daughter's March to the Sea

by Diane Gross
Warner Robins, Georgia

I must say that I have never been so swept off my feet as I was when my youngest daughter sent me an essay she had written for her college English class. Each time I read it, I cried. I want to share this story with others— so here is the story of my daughter's "March to the Sea."

A March Down to the Sea, an essay by Andrea Gross

"You sit on the suitcase while I try to zip it up," I said as I stuffed an extra pair of socks in at the last second. My little brother, overjoyed at the chance to be destructive, took a running start and jumped on top of my suitcase with an energetic, "Geronimo!"

This was to be a trip to remember, or at least, I was determined that it would be. Spring break of your senior year in high school happens only once, and I had one chance to make a memory that would last forever. Although I was going with my family to visit my sister in Saint Augustine, Florida, I was sure I could conjure up some unsupervised fun in the sun.

Early the next morning, I wearily opened one eye as the door of my room creaked open. My father, clad in an aroma of Old Spice, tiptoed up to my bed, which had not yet been visited by the light of day. With one fell swoop, he lifted me into his big arms and carried me to the ready-made bed in the van so that my brother and I could snooze away the wee hours of the morning. I was always secretly awake during this part, though I never let my father know it. There was just something about being sixteen and still getting carried to the car by your dad. As long as he thought I was sleeping, I was glad to still be Daddy's little girl.

My family had always been close. We seemed to have it all together. We even went to church every Sunday. Soon, however, our trip to the beach would change my life forever, in a way that I had never imagined.

On our second day at my sister Donna's house, she suggested that we do a Bible study together. This was not unusual for my family, so we gathered around the coffee table as she began to read from 1 Corinthians.

The words she spoke pierced my heart. Although it was not the first time I'd read the passage, somehow this was the first time I listened to what it said. She read, "Do not be deceived. Neither fornicators, nor idolaters, nor adulterers, nor homosexuals, nor sodomites, nor thieves, nor covetous, nor drunkards, nor revilers, nor extortioners will inherit the kingdom of God" (1 Corinthians 6:9–10 NKJV). My face suddenly felt hot. I swallowed hard in a vain attempt to smooth the lump in my throat.

A thought crossed my mind so loudly that I thought others might have heard it saying, *If that's true, then I have no hope.* I certainly had not been living my life by that standard, even though I called myself a Christian and went to church every Sunday. The next thing I knew, my eyes were filling up with tears. I pretended to sneeze so that I could wipe them away. Then, in the middle of my hopeless despair, she continued to read the next line (verse 11), saying: "And such were some of you. But you were washed, but you were sanctified, but you were justified in the name of the Lord Jesus and by the Spirit of our God." Those words were like a breath of fresh air to my condemned heart.

I knew I had to make a change. I had been living the life of a hypocrite, saying I knew God and yet I knew I did not. Church had been one thing to me, and my private life had been something else.

I decided, then and there, to beg for God's forgiveness and the strength to return home to a new life, for indeed, I felt like a new person. I finally understood the verse that says, "Therefore, if anyone is in Christ, he is a new creation; the old has gone, the new has come!" (2 Corinthians 5:17).

That day, on the beach at Saint Augustine, I marched down to the sea with my sins strapped on my back, and I unloaded them into the water. I held my breath and submerged myself in it. When I came up, I breathed freely for the first time in my life, having been baptized by God Himself in His mighty ocean. The spring break of my senior year blew my expectations out of the water. I had hoped it would be a memorable experience, and as I have now learned, God never leaves you disappointed.

—THE END—

My daughter's essay was her testimony, and it moved me beyond belief. When Andrea walked toward the ocean that afternoon so many years ago, neither Donna nor I understood what was going on. All three of us had been reading as we sat on our blanket on the beach, when Andrea simply and quietly got up and walked into the water until she was completely under. It scared me so badly I stood up, wondering whether to run to her or not. At the moment I stood in fear, she blasted joyfully out of the water, hands held high in the air. Then she just walked back out of the water, returning to our blanket with the giddy grin on her face of a child who knew a secret. I have told her often that she was a different girl after that day on the beach. I didn't realize until I read her essay that God had reached down into the sea and assured my daughter of His forgiveness and love, and none of us have been the same since!

Bandaging and Bailing

by Alyse A. Lounsberry
Heathrow, Florida

Patti and I hit it off instantly. We shared a love of antiques, flowers, and interior design. She ran a small booth at a nearby antiques mall where I worked part time for a friend. Ours was a friendship that involved one of God's U-turns.

Patti was married to Clark, a Christian who once had aspired to teach theology at the college level. Events and circumstances, however, had conspired to break his spirit, robbing him of the necessary zeal to realize that dream.

Spiritually speaking, Patti was in worse shape than Clark. She had gone to Tulsa, Oklahoma, to attend Bible school. A combination of misunderstandings and disappointments led to her being ostracized by leadership and asked to leave the school—which she gladly did. She left the school, all right, but she left the faith, too. She walked away from God that day and had never once looked back, except in pain and anger.

That is, until the day we sat staring at the packing crates piled up in the center of my living room, talking about my impending move to Dallas and how it had so quickly transpired. Patti may have thought the move had come up quickly, but God and I knew the truth. I had prayed my guts out for more than a year for a job in publishing. And here I was, prayers answered, about to move to Dallas to become an in-house editor at Word Publishing.

As we talked that afternoon, I knew I had to tread lightly on the topic of faith. Every time I mentioned prayer and its role in my life and future, Patti bristled. So I would mention my prayers and then pull back. Then I would refer to my faith and pull back again. Patti began to rail on angrily about how God had let her down and how mad she still was at Him when the still, small voice of the Holy Spirit whispered in my ear, *Tell her she may be mad at Me, but I was never mad at her!*

I sat there a moment, praying silently, until I was absolutely certain that He wanted me to speak those words to her.

In the middle of one of her tirades, I said, "God says to tell you that you may be mad at Him, but He was never mad at you!" Shocked speechless, she just looked at me blankly. I could see the words bore straight through the concrete wall she had built around her wounded heart.

"Patti," I said, "I am going to move away from here in just a matter of days. I want you to know that we can pray right now, this minute. You can return to Him. He's not angry with you. He never was. Patti, I promise that until I move, I will pray with you and study with you and encourage you until you get your feet back on the ground with Him."

With tears spilling from her eyes, Patti prayed a simple prayer of repentance.

"God, I repent for judging You and for my anger toward You. I thank You that You loved me right through the mess and that You were never mad at me. Thank You for receiving me back as Your child today. Amen."

We had lunch a few more times, read the Bible, and

prayed. She asked lots of questions, which I tried to answer from my own experience and study of the Word. Patti, it seemed, had become hungry again for the things of God. She was like a sponge, soaking up everything as if to make up for lost time. Gone was the woman I had first met.

Her renewed faith had acted as a tonic in the life of Clark, too. Together they began to attend a local church, which became a place of healing and recovery, deliverance and discovery.

About a year and a half after my move from Tulsa to Dallas, the phone rang. I was delighted to hear Patti's voice on the other end.

"How are you?" I asked.

"Not so good," she confided. "I have just been diagnosed with stage-four lymphoma."

Stunned, all I could think to ask was, "How many stages are there?"

"Four," was all she said.

"Oh, Patti! I am so sorry!"

"No," she said, "don't be. I am calling to thank you for getting me ready for all this. I called to thank you for getting me ready for heaven."

As I sobbed, she thanked me. Again and again, she mentioned how much she had learned about God's love for her in the past months since she made that U-turn back to Him.

"I know He loves me, and He's not punishing me with this," she told me. "But I also know I'm probably not going to make it. I'm going to fight like crazy to overcome this thing; but if I don't, I want you to know I'm ready to meet Him because you cared enough to get in my face with some words I didn't want to hear!"

Patti didn't make it, but her brightness of spirit and

courage in the middle of adversity were an inspiration to all around her. She touched many lives with the witness of her own life.

One of my own enduring images of Jesus is His "Samaritan" nature—His willingness to drop everything and get down into ditches alongside us, bandage us, and bail us out. He came for the broken ones among us, the brokenhearted, and those of us with shattered lives and dreams in shambles. When we need to recover and continue on the way, I envision Him bandaging and bailing, so that once again we can walk in wholeness and love. That's what He wants us to do for the "Pattis" among us—start bandaging and bailing until they are sufficiently healed to walk out in wholeness and love.

That's what Patti did for others right up until the day she died. She was an active and vital witness for Christ, always praising Him, always telling of His love and goodness and mercy. She told countless others how the Lord had taken her back even in her angry state and how He'd take them back, too.

It's never too late for any of us to make one of these critical U-turns with God. Whenever He hears our pitiful cries, He comes and starts the bandaging and bailing. He is merciful and full of grace.

Call Him. He will answer you.

The Ring

by Rose Sweet
Palm Desert, California
(for my niece, Kristin)

As a little girl I often dreamed of, and carefully planned, my wedding day.

I knew just how my dress would look and how the music would sound. Even with my eyes closed, I could see all the admiring faces that would be in church that day. I, who often felt lost in my family of seven, would finally be the center of attention.

I was raised in a Christian home and asked God into my heart at an early age. Attending church was comforting during my often chaotic childhood, where most of the time I felt like just another face that needed feeding. Mom and Dad married young, had come from troubled homes, and like so many of us who become parents at an early age, had hardly a clue about what they were doing. I knew they loved me, but I wanted a better life than they had. I was determined to chart my own course, no matter what they said. As soon as I hit my teens, the real trouble started.

Church activities and my relationship with God took a back burner to staying out on weeknights and sleeping in on weekends. I was seventeen, still living at home, and always butting heads with my mother. One day, though, in an effort to get on my mom's good side,

I dressed up, put on a genuinely cheerful attitude, and went with her to church. I was quite startled when a lady I hardly knew came right up to me and said, "Have you read Jeremiah 29:11?"

Of course I knew that Bible verse, so I casually answered, "Sure," even though I wanted to say, "Lady, what business is it of yours?" A few years later, her comment would come back to convict me.

When we don't live life God's way, things eventually fall apart. By now I was twenty and trapped in a dismal job, my parents were divorced, and my stepdad and I fought almost daily. I longed for a family of my own and a love that wouldn't fail me. At that low point in my life, I met Eric.

Eric was kind and handsome, and we could talk for hours. Who could resist that twinkle in his eye and the way he looked at me? Within a few short weeks, we were "in love," and it looked like my dream of that church wedding was coming true. Since I was not used to checking my choices with God's intentions for me, I began to make my own life plans around Eric. I was so intent on almost racing down that church aisle that I ignored the fact that Eric was stuck in the middle of a long, drawn-out divorce and had two small children. No problem; I would help him with the divorce, and I'd love his two kids. Never mind that he owed past-due child support; again I would help him. That's what wives do, right?

When emotions run high, the body soon follows. Before I knew it, I had traded my precious purity for sexual intimacy. I felt closer to Eric than ever, but farther than ever from my parents, and millions of miles away from God. I spent nights at Eric's house, cooking his dinners, washing his clothes, and playing "wife." It felt good. I ignored the thoughts that told me this was not the way it was supposed to be. Instead, I argued that a marriage license was just a piece of paper. I rationalized that we loved each other and, after all, who really needed a wedding? We were committed. Someday all the mess would be straightened out.

For the next three years, I gave my life and love to Eric and his children, who called me Mom. The bills still weren't paid, and the divorce problems lingered. Although Eric and I fought frequently, I was surprised that my old dream of a wedding never went away, so I began to push for a ring. Eric placed a sparkling diamond on my hand, and for awhile I again thought there would be a wedding. How naive we women often are, and how stubborn we can be! Kisses aren't contracts, and rings aren't always promises, but we refuse to see the truth. Just before Christmas Eric walked out, leaving me with a broken heart, a shattered soul, and a diamond ring that meant nothing.

The next Sunday, I drove around town looking for a new church where no one knew Eric or me. I was too ashamed to show my face to all my friends to whom I'd rationalized that we were "married in spirit." As I sat in the back pew, weighed down by shame and sadness, I heard the pastor preach on the old verse from Jeremiah 29:11: " 'For I know the plans I have for you,' declares the LORD, 'plans to prosper you and not to harm you, plans to give you hope and a future.' " I started sobbing as everything poured out of me. I knew I had taken a wrong turn a long time ago, and it was time to get back on the right path.

Scripture says God created us as masterpieces (Ephesians 2:10 NLT) and that He can renew us in Christ. If there's one thing I knew, I needed renewal! I took a good, hard look at my life and decided to "clean house" and get back into spiritual order.

Funny thing, when you're in the mood to throw out all the bad mental and emotional junk in your life, it helps to start by cleaning out the junk drawer in your kitchen! I rolled up my sleeves and began a mission to cast out all the clutter. With drawers open, countertops full, and bags of trash piling up, my heart stopped when I picked up the small velvet box that held my engagement ring. Instead of the sacred vows that diamond should represent, this ring meant only rejection. I knew what God wanted me to do with all my hurts, so I carefully cleaned the ring, put it back in the box, and sat down to write a note:

> *Dear God: I'm giving this ring to You, along with all the shame, anger, and hurt that go with it. I trust in Your time You will bring me a husband of Your choosing and that until then, You will provide for me.*
>
> > *Your daughter,*
> > *Kristin.*

I wrapped the velvet case with beautiful blue ribbon and stuck it with the note into my pocket. At church that morning, I secretly slipped the box into the offering basket, giving back to my heavenly Father all the things that had separated us for so long.

My U-turn journey back to God began that day, and I have never looked back.

Tea and Crackers

by Gail Hayes,
Durham, North Carolina

These days, I see God's love in the smallest things. One morning, while watching a praise and worship tape, I marveled as my two-year-old daughter worshiped the Lord. She blew on her toy clarinet, moving with the music, caught up in the wind of His power. It was simply beautiful. The Lord immersed me in the flood of His love with my baby. Looking at this scene, it was hard to believe that it was not so long ago that the thought of having a child made me cringe.

As the firstborn girl of seven, the last thing I wanted was a child. I helped my mother with my siblings, and during my young adulthood all I wanted was complete freedom. I wanted freedom to do what I wanted, when I wanted, and how I wanted. Then suddenly my freedom collided with the brick wall of my actions' consequences. At age twenty-two, I was unmarried and pregnant.

I did not know the Lord and decided to terminate the pregnancy. I wanted that parasite out of my body. Yes, I called the life growing within me a parasite. I hated myself, so how could I feel anything for this child? I entered the abortion clinic, wanting a quick and easy solution to my problem. The counselor was all too happy to explain that this was not a human life but merely a glob of tissue the needed to be cleaned out of my body. This would be a simple procedure, she said.

She took my money, covered my fear with smiles, and undressed me with deceit. I submitted myself and "this glob" to the abortionist's hand. Afterward, I was served tea and crackers. I ate, not realizing the high price I would later pay for that snack.

I felt great relief as I exited the clinic, vowing never to go through its doors again. In a few months, I moved away from the Washington, D.C., area, hoping to start a new life, not realizing the devastating blow I had dealt to my body and spirit.

I had moved back home to live with my parents and attend school when shortly thereafter I discovered I was pregnant again. Once again I had made a wrong turn, and once again I went to an abortionist. The results of this visit were a suicide attempt and a deep self-loathing I would be unable to shake for many years. This was payment for my second helping of tea and crackers.

Years later, after receiving the Lord, I discovered that I was grieving for those lost children. I turned to the Lord, and He did something miraculous for me. I fell on my face before Him and asked Him to open my womb. After eleven years of being barren, within two months of that prayer, I discovered I was pregnant. In my forties, He restored my lost children to me. Tears of unspeakable joy fill my eyes when tiny arms encircle my neck. With each hug, fragments of yesterday's torment vanish. With each kiss, healing balm fills my once-broken heart.

This is the depth of His love. He restored everything taken by the darkness of my past. He shined His light on the hidden treasures buried in my soul and gave me a future and a hope. He enveloped me in the sea of His love and washed me in the wave of His awesome forgiveness.

My cup overflows with promises for my future. He anointed me with oil, draped me in royal robes, and placed a crown upon my head. I am His daughter, a daughter of the King.

His Word says He removes our sin far from us. Because of His mercy, I stand unashamed of my past. Because of His loving-kindness, I pray for those caught in abortion's deadly trap. I pray that like me, they will one day stand in the flow of God's love and not consume another snack of tea and crackers. Today, I stand waiting to wipe fear's crumbs from hurting mouths and to dry lips dripping with guilt's tea. I stand waiting to love someone into the kingdom.

Chapter Two

A Mother's Love

And this is my prayer:
that your love may abound
more and more in knowledge and depth of insight.

Philippians 1:9

Clown Love

by Candace Carteen,
Battleground, Washington

Jean Carteen was ready to give up on God and all her beliefs in a Holy Spirit. She had gotten pregnant five times, and not one of those babies had been able to call her "Mommy." She carried the first until she was five months along. The second self-aborted at four months. The third was born dead at eight months, and the fourth only made it to the third month of pregnancy. The doctors couldn't tell Jean why this was happening. All her siblings had at least five children each. But her nest was empty.

When she got pregnant the fifth time, she didn't hold much faith that this child would make it into the world alive either. Each month she said a silent, tempered prayer that she would get to hold and love and watch this one grow up, but a little piece of her no longer believed that prayer worked in her life.

At age fourteen, she knew she wanted to be a mommy. After marrying at fifteen, she figured it would be easy to get pregnant. She was correct! Two months later, she was pregnant. Soon after, she wasn't. A year after that, she was pregnant again. Then she wasn't. Between the loss of their children and the dysfunction of the marriage, the young couple soon divorced.

Jean remarried a couple years later. In this marriage,

two babies were also lost. After thirteen childless years of marriage, Jean and her second husband divorced and went their separate ways.

Jean then met John. He was good to her, and they had what she described as "a happy and loving marriage." Three months after their honeymoon, she was pregnant. She didn't tell anyone, including her husband, for the first three months. She figured, "Why? This won't last."

The third month came and went, and she was still pregnant. The fourth, fifth, sixth, seventh, and eighth months came and went, and she was still pregnant. She could feel the baby moving and kicking her. She had gained sixty pounds, was rotund and basking in guarded happiness.

One evening, toward the last days of her pregnancy, she brought her hands together in prayer and spoke the words that she had been afraid to say sooner.

"God, please bless this child. It looks like You have finally decided that I will become a mommy. Thank You! I give this child to You to watch over and protect. Amen."

The little voice inside her head finally told her it was time to believe and do something to tell her heart that this was real. There was going to be a child to hold and love and care for.

Jean's belly became a wonderful working table as she sat down on the soft couch, where she sacrificed a pair of her husband's new white socks and a colorful old dress she no longer wore. She then gathered together some bright scraps of felt she had left from the Christmas decorations and borrowed a needle and thread from a neighbor. Her fertile mind started to design and redesign the materials until she knew, in her mind's eye, exactly what the finished product was going to look like.

With the dexterity of a pianist, her nimble fingers

twisted and turned the materials as she tacked here and stitched there. A big, bulbous black nose, two bright blue eyes, a huge red grin, and two elephant-sized ears made up the head. Long, wiry sock arms and legs were stitched ever so precisely to a sock body. Ruffles appeared from the sleeves of the dress, and ballooning legs were cut from the dress's hem. When she was through meshing the materials together, Jean had fashioned a smiling clown doll.

It was then time to stuff the soft shell, but she found nothing suitable around the old, bare, one-bedroom shack. It suddenly dawned on her that there was a cotton field across the street that had been seeded but not picked. She wrestled a pillowcase off the pillow on her side of the bed, tucked a small step stool under her arm, and waddled across the quiet, dusty road. Looking out over the field, she felt completely overwhelmed. She took a deep breath and brought her hands together in prayer.

"Dear God, please give me the strength to pull enough cotton to finish this project."

She stroked her enormous stomach and continued. "I just have to have this finished before this little one comes out of this big belly. Amen, God!"

She felt a sudden rush of calmness come over her body and mind as she set the stool down between the clouds of cotton and started to pull the soft centers out of the tough hulls. Wad after wad was stuffed into the pillowcase. When the case was as plump as her belly, she eased herself off the stool and toddled home with the sack swung over her shoulder, like a department store Santa after a long day's work.

"Thank You, God," she whispered as she finally entered the abode.

Jean poured herself a tall glass of water, carried it

over to the chair where she had placed her loot, set it on the side table, and tucked her larger-than-normal bottom in a big, overstuffed chair. For the next several hours, she removed the seeds and leftover husks from the cotton. As the last piece was plucked clean, she finished her water and fell asleep.

John came home and found her slumped over in the big easy chair. Instead of waking her, he placed a warm blanket around her maternal body and went to bed.

In the middle of the night, Jean awoke and continued her project. She retrieved two metal-toothed dog brushes from the side table drawer and started combing the cotton into small fluffy battings. She then placed the limp clown's body on her belly-table and started stuffing the doll.

The next morning when John awoke, he discovered Jean fast asleep and "Jolly John, the Clown" smiling from atop her belly.

A few hours later, Jean went into labor, and a baby girl was born.

I was that baby girl.

This clown, crafted with a mother's prayer, slept with me until I was in my late teens. It now sits on my son's dresser—a constant reminder of the love God had for Jean and the blessing of a baby girl for whom God provided a wonderful mother.

Not Just Any Serviceman

by Betty Winslow,
Bowling Green, Ohio

A shorter version of this story appeared in Guideposts, *October 1999.*

I was thrilled when my daughter Lisa was appointed to the U.S. Naval Academy's Class of 1994. As a lifelong supporter of the military, I remembered the stories my dad, a WWII navy veteran, used to tell about how important mail call was. He said that days with no mail can make a serviceman feel forgotten and unappreciated. After Lisa left for Annapolis, I began a steady stream of letters, cards, and care packages rolling her way, a stream which continued for almost four years.

But in December of her last year at USNA, tragedy struck. A carload of midshipmen returning from that year's Army/Navy football game was crushed when a rain-soaked rotten willow tree crashed across the highway and over their car, less than a mile from the academy. Three girls died. One of them was Lisa. There would be no more letters going out filled with news of home, no more care packages of cookies and candy to be shared with classmates, no more jokes and cartoons to make a frazzled midshipman and her friends laugh.

As a freelance writer, I would continue to write, but my favorite assignment was over. I was no longer "Mailmom."

Several years later, I saw a "Dear Abby" column in the newspaper asking people to write to servicemen over the holidays. I said to myself, "If it were my daughter away from home at Christmas and being forgotten at mail call, I'd want someone to write to her." It would be hard, I knew, to write letters to unknown faces, but I thought about how much Lisa and her friends had enjoyed my letters, and I knew I had to do it.

I sat down and slowly began to write. The letter was long and newsy and it introduced me, my hometown, and my family in as entertaining a way as possible. I thought about not including Lisa's part in my life. Would it make the recipient too sad? She was a big part of what had made me who I was today and why I was doing this, so I knew I needed to at least mention her. Briefly, carefully, I wrote about her life, her years at USNA, and her tragic death, praying all the while that God would use it to bless, not hurt, the ones who received my letters.

Before her death, Lisa had been looking forward to being commissioned as a Marine Corps officer, so I especially wanted my letters to go to lonely Marines. To make sure they did, I decorated five envelopes with rubber stamped bears playing "The Marine Corps Hymn" on bugles and addressed each of them to "Any Serviceman (USMC)." I then stuck a copy of my letter in each envelope and dropped them all in the mail. I didn't expect any answers; servicemen are notorious for wanting mail and always finding time to read it, but they seldom seem to find time to answer it!

My letters ended up on the USS *Guam*. Two young

Marines from the battalion stationed aboard chose envelopes from the "Operation Dear Abby" mailbag to fill their time. One chose mine because the town in my return address was near his Michigan hometown, the other because he got a kick out of the bugle-playing bears I'd put on the envelope. Returning to the room they shared, they were surprised to discover they'd both chosen letters from the same woman.

Then, as they began to read, they discovered another surprise: the woman who'd written their randomly chosen letters was the mother of their late USNA classmate, Lisa. Thrilled, they immediately wrote back, sharing memories of Lisa and telling me how much it had meant to them, so close to the date of her death, to receive news that Lisa's family was well.

Several years later, another classmate of Lisa's wrote that he, too, had received an "Any Serviceman (USMC)" letter from me that Christmas and that it had meant so much to him that he still had it.

My letters may have been addressed to "Any Serviceman," but God knew their names—and mine.

Doing the Dishes with Mom

by Rev. Michael F. Welmer,
Houston, Texas

Before the days when we could afford a dishwasher, Mom and I would stand at the kitchen sink and "do the dishes." That is how Mom always referred to it. What we were doing to them I don't know. What it was doing to me was life-altering.

One of the first memories I have about it is that it was never a chore. Mom always made doing the dishes an act of love and service. She never complained or griped. Time after time, Mom refused the help of guests.

"The dishes will keep," she'd say.

Yes, the dishes will keep. They will keep a very treasured secret! Over the years I learned to cherish doing the dishes with Mom and the insights into life this simple rite revealed.

Doing the dishes with Mom was a cleansing process, not just for the dishes, but also for me. I talked; she listened. No interference. No judgment. It was good therapy. Mom taught me the value of confession. I would disclose my feelings, frustrations, hurts, and joys with her. She would impart her love, care, compassion, concern, and counsel.

We watched the world through the window over

the sink. We eyed the traffic and the neighbors. We watched the seasons change and the weather rage. Mom consistently found a reason to direct my gaze outside the window. Mom taught me to look beyond myself to others around me and the world about me.

I hated to dry and stack the dishes. I always wanted to wash them. Mom taught me to do the things I hate. Doing the dishes with Mom taught me to take turns.

All of those lessons—service, confession, cleansing, doing what I don't like to do, and taking turns—God used to prepare me for my life as a husband, father, friend, and shepherd of His people.

Now sainted at the Lord's right hand, Mom doesn't do the dishes, but I still do. It is my therapy. It is a way for me to summon up the precious life-forming lessons my mom taught me. It is the mechanism I use to center my life and my ministry. And it is a way for me to visit with Mom once more.

Chapter Three

Tales of Triumph

I know what it is to be in need,
and I know what it is to have plenty.
I have learned the secret of being content
in any and every situation,
whether well fed or hungry,
whether living in plenty or in want.
I can do everything through him who gives me strength.

Philippians 4:12–13

A Matter of Perspective

by Maie Kellerman,
Bright's Grove, Ontario,
Canada

If it's true that God gives special-needs children to exceptional people, then He knew what He was doing when He lent Justin to Kathryn.

Kathryn was a remarkable youngster with a gift for radiating love and happiness and a soft spot for tiny babies. I remember her mother commenting during her early teens that Kathryn had two passions in life: boys and babies. "Heaven forbid that she works out the logical connection between the two prematurely," she laughed. Kathryn grew into an enchanting, intelligent young woman, married (too young), and was blessed, at a respectable interval after the nuptials, by Justin's birth.

Justin did his mother proud. He soon demonstrated the same delight in his world that she had for hers. The only blight on Kathryn's happiness was her babe's ongoing, seemingly innocuous, digestive problems. Unpleasant as Justin's vomiting attacks were, no one was particularly perturbed by them until, during his sixteenth month, an attack continued for more than a day. He was admitted to a hospital, where a scan revealed a brain tumor. The orange-sized monstrosity was excised. It was malignant.

Worse still, the cancer was rare. Only ten cases had been reported worldwide and it is apparently intractable.

To suggest that Kathryn was not devastated by the diagnosis would be to deny her intelligence and fundamental realism. Yet her faith that her baby would survive was unshakable. She remained upbeat and optimistic that Justin would be the first to beat this disease. Kathryn was not to be supported in this battle by her young husband. His inherent shallowness was manifested in his shockingly callous admonishment to her to "accept that the kid's going to die, Kath. And don't expect me to mourn a child I never wanted anyway."

The young man's attitude never changed, so it was no surprise when, some time after the events of this story, they separated.

I remember well my first meeting with Justin after his operation. He was leading his mother around the yard in gentle, drunken circles. (A consequence of the removal of the tumor was significant loss of motor skills.) He greeted me with glee and explained that he was "showing Mum the flowers." They entertained each other and the assembled family with their inconsequential nonsense while practicing walking.

Lunch was a normally messy affair, with Justin insisting on feeding his great-aunt corn by hand. What struck me most about this and many days thereafter was how much fun it had been. There was no feeling of a lament playing offstage, reminding us of the fact that Justin was living on borrowed time. No one was determinedly cheerful. The family gathering was, as always, a noisy, rollicking affair.

Kathryn befriended a number of people she met on the pediatric oncology ward, in particular, Jeannine, whose son, Tyler, was battling another type of brain cancer. It's hard to imagine how it must feel to watch your child, who is too young to understand what is being done to him or why he must undergo it, being subjected to the rigors of chemotherapy.

Jeannine did not cope well. Kathryn tried to buoy her with her own optimism and belief in life. Both babies suffered frequent setbacks during the next few months. Justin's tumor reemerged and required another operation. Tyler's malignancy at first seemed unresponsive to chemotherapy. Jeannine needed and received a great deal of support through each of Tyler's setbacks. What Kathryn found trying, however, was Jeannine's overwrought reaction to Justin's trials.

"Aren't you terrified that he'll die, Kath? What are you going to do if the next treatment doesn't work?"

Even when Tyler's tumor disappeared and the doctors declared his prognosis to be excellent, Jeannine could not let go of her fear.

One day, Kathryn confided in me. "Jeannine and I," she said, "both have sons with cancer. Her son's prognosis is good—not perfect but very, very good. Justin's is not good. Either Tyler or Justin could die tomorrow. Or they could live to bury the pair of us. There's just one big difference between our stories. If Justin dies tomorrow, I will have had two wonderful years with a wonderful small boy. If Tyler dies tomorrow, Jeannine will have had a tragedy."

I was profoundly moved by this insight and forced to reexamine my own perceptions about this particular drama and so much of my own life.

Eventually, once Justin's tumor reached gross proportions for a third time, and on the advice of her oncologist, Kathryn decided she was unwilling to subject the mite to further treatment. Her decision was made with the same grace and dignity she had shown all along.

Justin apparently enjoyed his second birthday party, although by then the painkillers made him dopey, and he catnapped frequently. Photographs captured him fast asleep, clutching a piece of cake, surrounded by his boisterous small friends. A month later, he died. Tears flowed freely at Justin's funeral. The church was packed with family and friends, including two nurses who had, on their own time, spelled Kathryn around the clock in caring for Justin for the last few weeks. But, fittingly, the talk after the service was about the great kid Justin had been, his cute sayings and ways, the indelible stamp he'd left on those he had encountered.

Kathryn had had two wonderful years with a wonderful son, not a tragedy, and that blessed gift from God is what she, and many of us who knew Justin, will always remember.

finally a father's Love

by Gloria Cassity Stargel,
Gainesville, Georgia

While the family waited in Joe's hospital room, hours dragged by, and there was still no word from surgery. "Why is it taking so much time?" I kept asking of no one in particular. Fear of losing my husband ignited within me such a sense of anxiety—of insecurity—that it rekindled long-suppressed memories.

All at once, I am again a little six-year-old girl, terrified and alone. That night, my father had come home on yet another drunken rampage. As usual, concerned for our safety, Mother and we five children scattered like scared rabbits—using any avenue for escape.

I clambered out a bedroom window, dropping to the ground into a frightful darkness. On hands and knees, I groped my way under the house—spiderwebs hitting me in the face and sticking to my hair. I felt near panic at the thought of what else might be crawling under there. At long last, I reached Mother, who was waiting on the other side.

"Sh-h-h-h," she cautioned.

With the quilts she kept stashed away for those times, we fled to a neighbor's cornfield. There we spent most of the night, until all got quiet inside the house—no more furniture breaking, no more loud streams of profanity. Then, hoping that Daddy had at last collapsed into a deep sleep, we dared creep back inside to our beds.

The next day I went to school and tried to pretend everything was normal.

Before I reached fifth grade, Mother managed somehow to move us across the state, away from Daddy's abuse. For the first time in my life, I could attend Sunday school. I quickly learned to love this Jesus person they talked about. But I couldn't believe He loved me. Having never experienced a father's nurturing love, I didn't even understand the concept.

As a result, I grew up battling an inferiority complex. I constantly sought love, approval. When I met Joe, dependable and hardworking, I knew he was a man I could trust. We fell in love and married soon after I turned eighteen. We had no money, but our security was in each other. We had the same goals—a house and children. A real home.

Now, years later back in Joe's hospital room, I faced the possibility of losing all that. Randy was away at college, Rick was to leave that fall, and Joe lay unconscious somewhere—facing I knew not what. Somebody had yanked my security rug out from under me. I was falling. . .falling. . . "Please, God, help!"

Suddenly the waiting was over. With the green surgical mask hanging loosely around his neck, Dr. Brown entered the room. He didn't need to say a word. Again his eyes told the story. I wanted to cry.

"We removed a malignant mass," he said. Cancer! My worst fear had become a reality!

Groping for reassurance, I asked, "Did you get it all?"

He answered a soft, "No, we just couldn't."

That's when it happened. I felt myself begin to reel,

too weak to reach out even to God. But God, in His divine love, reached down to me. I was aware of His presence in that room. Emanating from a haze at the ceiling, two mighty arms appeared, arms swathed in sleeves of a flowing white robe. The powerful yet gentle hands opened toward me as if to say, "Come, let Me help you. You don't have to be strong, Gloria. I'll be strong for you. Lean on Me."

I fell into those arms and stayed. Whereupon I was lifted up and above all that was going on in my world. For months, I was to remain in a state of almost suspended animation, protected like a chrysalis attached to a limb.

When we went home from the hospital, the cancer thing went with us, along with a six-months-to-live prognosis. Joe underwent extremely sickening chemotherapy, then debilitating radiation treatments. I fulfilled my role as wife and caregiver. Yet, I observed all this action from my high vantage point. I was an onlooker to a scenario that involved someone who looked just like me. And even though I wept and worried, in my heart burned a flicker of hope for Joe's healing.

All the while, so touched was I by the Lord's coming to me in my hour of need, I sought to know Him better. Once Joe could be up and about, a typical morning found me sitting in the den, surrounded by my Bible, a notebook and pen, inspirational books by Catherine Marshall, Andrew Murray, and Billy Graham. . .even the hymnbook.

In my readings, I discovered many evidences of God's love for us, even for me. I found accounts of Jesus' miracles of healing, not just in New Testament days, but today! I gulped those life-giving truths like a man dying of thirst who comes upon an oasis.

In those quiet times, I poured out my heart to God.

Then I learned to sit quietly and hear Him. And although I trusted God for the end result, I admit to some serious begging for Joe's life.

Slowly but surely, like a rosebud opening up to the sun, my soul opened up to the Son. And as it did, hope filled me, filled me to overflowing. I took a determined hold on faith, shifting my emphasis from medicine to God as the ultimate Healer. On those days when doubts crept in, I sang with gusto, "Have faith in God, He's on His throne. . . ." *And if He is on His throne*, I told myself, *He has control of this world, Joe, and me.*

Finally, we reached the one-year-since-cancer mark. Joe's treatments were behind us, at least for the time being. All at once, it was as if the Lord stood me back on my feet with a pat on the shoulder. "You'll be okay now." The first thing I noticed was that the sun was shining.

We waited anxiously for a pardon from Joe's cancer-caused death sentence—always conscious of the physician's grim prediction, "It will come back." Joe urged me to further my education so I could earn a living, just in case. Following much prayer for guidance, I returned to college—a first-quarter sophomore—after an absence of twenty-seven years!

Many months of study later, it is graduation day at Brenau College. On front campus for the outdoor ceremony, faculty and dignitaries in full academic regalia take their places on the platform. While I—wearing black robe with gold-tasseled mortarboard atop my head, sporting a shiny blue-stoned class ring on my finger and a mile-wide grin on my face—line up with the other graduating seniors, most of them the ages of my children.

When I hear my name echo among the vintage oaks, this newly free butterfly, wings unfurled, fairly floats down the aisle to receive her heretofore-undreamed-of award—

Bachelor of Science degree in social work/journalism. And, by the grace of God, there to witness the auspicious occasion is—Joe.

So what happened after this butterfly soared free? I set about to become the writer God had called me to be—to share His undying love with a hurting world. Twenty-five years later, I still write. It is one way I can show my gratitude for Joe's miraculous healing. I remember the tenth-anniversary year of his surgery and the original "no hope" prognosis. His oncologist said, "Joe, I think we'll tell the computer you're well." How we savor each day together!

Meanwhile, I still soar with butterflies. But sometimes, I just enjoy being a little child again, confidently reaching for the hand of my heavenly Father. Always, He is there.

Arthur's Alterations

by Susi Redmond as told to
Mark L. Redmond,
South Bend, Indiana

When I was twenty-five, my life had been going basically the way I planned it. After graduating from high school in Kingston, Tennessee, I attended Tennessee Temple College. At the end of my junior year, I married a young man from Ohio. Mark and I planned to have four children and serve God for the rest of our lives.

After graduating in 1975, we both taught in a Christian school in Kingston for a year. Disillusioned, Mark quit teaching. We moved to Murfreesboro, Tennessee, where he worked for a publisher. When Mark returned to teaching in January 1978, his classroom was in South Bend, Indiana. I was homesick, but we were still serving the Lord.

By this time, I was temporarily out of the classroom because we had a two-year-old son, Benjamin. Although slightly disrupted by the move to Indiana, my life plan remained intact; Melody arrived in December 1978, right on time, according to our plan.

Shortly after Melody's birth, "Arthur" came along and demolished my plans. Arthur is the name we gave to the rheumatoid arthritis that attacked my body in 1979. There was no specialist for my disease in South Bend at the time. My doctor and the hospital where I spent two months were three hours away, in Kalamazoo, Michigan. Mark continued to teach and (at my request) visited me only on weekends. My parents kept our kids in Tennessee. Those two months were filled with the worst pain I had ever experienced. Before any treatment could be prescribed, a myriad of tests were run in an attempt to diagnose the disease.

Before entering the hospital, I had been an active, healthy, athletic twenty-five-year-old woman. When I returned home, I had arthritis in every joint and was practically bedridden. My doctor explained that several treatments were available that would put my disease in remission. I had hope, but I had no idea that Arthur would be so difficult to control.

Arthur's alterations in my life have been two-sided. Pain has been constant, sometimes nearly unbearable. I've endured lengthy hospital stays, painful shots, and medicines that caused stomach ulcers and mouth sores. I've dealt with chemotherapy, hair loss, stomach upset, fluid retention, and weight gain. There even was a brief time when my facial muscles froze in a ghastly grin because I had an allergic reaction to medication.

I made the three-hour trip to Kalamazoo dozens of times. Once, I even made the journey in an ambulance. That night I nearly died from toxic shock syndrome. Another time I was rushed to a local hospital when a low potassium level set off seizures. Then there were migraine headaches. They increased in intensity and frequency until the Friday after Thanksgiving 1996. The migraine headache that came that day stayed. Doctors tried everything they could think of to break it, but nothing worked until three years later when a Tennessee neurologist used a nerve block. My veins had been ruined by an earlier attempt by another doctor.

Two years ago, I developed an infection in a major artery near my heart. It nearly killed me.

But there's another side to Arthur's alterations. I do not have a "religion." I have a deep personal relationship with God. Nothing less could have sustained me and given me joy for the past twenty-three years.

When I was no longer able to cook for my family, our church congregation set up a schedule so that meals were prepared and delivered to our house three nights each week. I have rarely been able to attend church for the past five or six years; consequently, a number of the women who cooked for us regularly had never even met me.

Ladies from the church have cleaned our house repeatedly over the years. Several years ago, our church's "Can-Do Crew" remodeled and redecorated our bedroom. There was never any cost to our family.

In 1987, when I was still able to drive, someone noticed that our 1979 VW Rabbit with its standard transmission and lack of power steering was very difficult for me to drive. On Easter Sunday, the congregation presented us with a new car, complete with fully paid license plates and insurance. For six or seven years, an anonymous friend supplemented our income with weekly contributions of $100 because I couldn't work.

As our two children grew up, we cried together many times; but we also laughed, prayed, and loved. I remember a preschool Melody who, confused about being politically correct, asked, "Mom, are you handicapped or retarded?"

Another time, my English teacher husband made me laugh when I thought I had no laughter left in me. At a particularly bad time when I had taken about all the pain I could stand, he knelt beside our bed.

"I wish I was dead," I whispered.

"I wish I were dead," he said. "You need the subjunctive mood."

Our son is a youth pastor. He and his precious wife, Patti, have given us our grandchild, Kayla. They are among our closest friends. Melody, now a twenty-two-year-old college senior, attends classes at Indiana University South Bend. While many of her friends left to attend out-of-state Christian colleges, Melody chose to stay home because she wanted to help her father take care of me. She is my friend as well as my daughter.

Speaking of friends, I cannot close my story without including my best friend and faithful husband, Mark. Before Arthur arrived, Mark was immature, quick-tempered, negative, and sarcastic. There were times when I seriously doubted the wisdom of my decision to marry him. There definitely were times when I didn't like him. Through the years, however, God used Arthur to transform Mark.

There is nothing he won't do for me. Although he has never attended medical school, Mark has been my nurse, tending to tasks such as changing the dressing on an IV site. He has showered me with cards, flowers, and poetry, and continues to tell me that he thinks I'm beautiful. He has kept a candy dish and glass of ice water full and within my reach, held my hand, and put his arms around me when I hurt. Often he cries with me because there is nothing else he can do.

When I look back at the plan I had for myself, I find that my life has been drastically altered from where I thought it would be by the age of forty-seven. Many of my dreams will never become realities. Discouragement and depression will always be knocking on my door. But when I look around, I see that my God has directed my life to follow His plan. He has brought into my life people whom I otherwise would not have met. He has used me to influence and minister to people whom I might not otherwise have been able to help. And although this place where God has brought me is not comfortable, it is good to be here because He is here, too.

The Grasshopper

by Eva Marie Everson,
Casselberry, Florida

Reprinted with permission from Pinches of Salt, Prisms of Light *by Eva Marie Everson and Carmen Leal, Essence Publishers, 1999, and* One True Vow *by Eva Marie Everson, Promise Press, 2001.*

I spotted the grasshopper on an outside window ledge. Throughout the morning I watched him, basking in the warm sunshine, his wings periodically quivering in the gentle breeze.

Near noon, as the January wind started to increase, the grasshopper stirred from his resting place. As he inched his way up the tempered glass, I noticed that one of his back legs was missing.

His antennae worked furiously, guiding him. Inch by inch, push by push, with only five legs and the wind force against him, he finally reached his goal. Awhile later, he was satisfied with his victory and I watched as he returned to the ledge.

I was reminded of when we'd moved to Florida, six years earlier, to take advantage of a business opportunity for my husband. At the time of the move, we considered it a most wonderful gift from God. Then it became what seemed to be a curse from the enemy.

Eight months after the move, my husband and I

stared at a letter informing us that we had placed our "faith" in a farce. In a moment that is difficult to describe, our lives changed forever, as did our social position. We went from having the world by the tail to the imminent danger of watching everything we'd worked for slip through our fingers.

In all honesty, I don't think we truly realized the full impact of the situation. Within months, our savings were drained. We were forced to cash in our life insurance policies and IRAs. We sold some of our possessions and moved into a small, two-bedroom apartment with a fraction of the space we'd had a year earlier. We even filed for bankruptcy, hoping it would help get us back on our feet. And, finally, in our darkest hour, we requested government assistance in the form of welfare and food stamps.

The minutes in each day stretched into hours, and days of unending listlessness stretched into weeks. Though today I ask God to keep me from ever going through the experience again, this was the time of my life when incredible miracles took place.

My husband and I had always been the "givers." I'm not speaking just in terms of tithing but in giving to others, the needy. I'd always assumed that receiving a gift was easy. It's not. It's uncomfortably humbling. There were many days when I walked to our mailbox, praying to God about how we were going to pay the rent or the electric bill. I'd nearly collapse to my knees when I'd find an unexpected check, given to help us meet our needs. There were times when I stood before the open refrigerator, staring into its white barrenness and praying, "Lord, exactly what are the plans for dinner tonight? We have no food. Yet, You said Your seed would never be forsaken or beg for bread. What would

You have me do here?" Often, before I could close the refrigerator door, the phone would ring. "Just wanted to see if you were free for dinner tonight. We're buying." It happened time and again.

One afternoon, a friend called and asked if she could come over. I sensed by the tone of her voice that she had an agenda.

"Certainly," I answered.

When she arrived, we sat on the sofa, side by side, while she shared with me that she'd recently been "blessed" financially. "I wanted to share part of it with you," she continued, slipping a sealed envelope toward me. I was speechless, but words weren't necessary.

With all the miracles—too numerous to list in this limited space—there is one that stands above them all: the miracle that took place inside my heart. Never had I clung to the Word of God as I did during that trial. Never had I felt His comforting hand on my shoulder as I felt it then. I felt His wisdom growing inside of me, forming me into what He had always desired for me.

The defining moment came one brisk, winter morning. Weeks earlier, I'd seen an outfit in a boutique window that just had my name all over it. Oh, how I wanted it! It was me! A year earlier, I'd have bought it and thought nothing of it. But at this point in time, I didn't have enough to shop at a thrift store, much less an upscale boutique. That morning I saw my husband's ex-business partner's wife wearing the outfit. I cried all the way home, begging God to explain this to me.

"Isn't it enough that I'm down on my knees? Does life have to kick me in the gut, too?" I cried in agony.

I nearly ran into our apartment. As I bolted the door behind me, the phone rang. It was my dear, dear friend, Donald. "Hey, honey," he greeted me in his usual way.

"Listen, I don't know why. . .but God has impressed on me the need to tell you this. It doesn't matter what you drive, where you live, how much money you have, or what clothes you wear. What matters is that you trust Him."

This was more than just a moment of truth for me. It was the ultimate act of salt and light in my life. Donald received a message meant for him to give to me, and he followed through with what God told him to do. It was the message I needed to change my heart. From that moment, although wounded and battered like the grasshopper, I turned my faith upward and began the road toward perfection.

I won't achieve it in this lifetime. But I'm on the road. I'm going toward my destination. With my face to the wind, I can see the prize. I know with certainty that regardless of the ensuing difficulties, life is a most wonderful gift from God. I lost a lot; but, oh, look what I've gained!

Chapter Four

Children Are a Gift

When Jesus saw this, he was indignant. He said to them,
"Let the little children come to me, and do not hinder them,
for the kingdom of God belongs to such as these.
I tell you the truth, anyone who will not receive the kingdom
of God like a little child will never enter it."
And he took the children in his arms,
put his hands on them and blessed them.

Mark 10:14–16

A Woman's Journey

What Was I Supposed to Be?

by Lanita Bradley Boyd,
Fort Thomas, Kentucky

Published under the title: "What Happens to the Baby?"
in Portrait, *Autumn 1993,* The Turning Point, *Fall 1992,*
and The Christian Reader, *September/October 1992.*

I squinted against the glare of oncoming headlights.
Why was I so foolish to keep a seven-year-old up late on a
school night? I thought. Was the forty-five-mile drive to
hear a Christian concert worth it? I was tired and sleepy
and questioning my parental judgment. I glanced at
Kelsey to see if she was asleep. Eyes bright, she was
obviously not as drowsy as I was.

"Mom, what was that song about with all the pictures of the doctor's stuff and teacher's stuff and children and old people and the baby's hand at the end?"

I had to think. Several of the concert's songs were
accompanied by slides. Then I remembered.

"Do you mean, 'What Was I Supposed to Be?' " I
asked.

"Yes, that's it. What did that mean?"

I took a deep breath. I was wide awake now, praying quickly my explanation would be complete and yet
not too frightening for her. Hesitantly, I began.

"Honey, sometimes girls get pregnant when they aren't married." I could tell by her look I was already in trouble.

"But how can they do that? I thought getting married was how you had babies."

"Well," I groped, "sometimes teenagers do things before they are married—well, they act like—well, they do with each other's body what married people do. Then the girl gets pregnant. When she does, she has various choices."

I took a breath. "The girl and boy can get married if they love each other. A lot of people do that. Sometimes it works out to be a good marriage, and sometimes it doesn't.

"The girl and her parents can keep the baby and take care of it. Or the girl can give it up for adoption." I paused, considering my next words. "The way your birth mother did you."

Kelsey brought me back to the point. "I still don't understand the song."

"The other choice is called abortion. That's when a doctor uses instruments inside the girl—a type of surgery—to get rid of the baby when it is still very tiny."

The voice beside me was also tiny. "Then what happens to the baby?"

"It's gone. The hospital gets rid of it, and the girl goes home. She isn't pregnant anymore." I hoped I was telling Kelsey what she could hear and comprehend.

"The song was written from the baby's viewpoint," I continued. "The baby was asking Jesus what it would have been if it had lived to be born. It said, 'What was I supposed to be? What were my eyes supposed to see? Why did I taste of death before I even drew a breath, hid my head at my mother's breast to sleep? O Jesus, what was I supposed to be?' "

I had no idea whether any of this was making sense to my little traveling companion until I heard her shuddering breath. I glanced over to see tears streaming from her eyes. She caught her breath in short puffs.

Finally, she whispered, "Then that's what my birth mother could have done to me if she hadn't loved me so much?"

I eased the car to the side of the highway and stopped. I took Kelsey in my arms. We sobbed and stroked each other—and loved each other even more than before.

This gift of love from an unknown birth mother had changed my life forever. Tonight this song had made my little daughter aware for the first time of one of the greatest gifts of love—the gift of life.

A Woman's Journey

On My Honor

by Anne Goodrich,
Kalamazoo, Michigan

When the door to our small mobile home swung open the afternoon of September 11, I was already home. Earlier that day, my boss had immediately said, "Go" when I told him I wanted to be home when my eleven-year-old son arrived from school. I had driven home under a pristine blue sky that looked surreal compared to the images in my mind of the terrorist attacks on the World Trade Center and the Pentagon.

Suddenly, the door swung open and my son was there, curious why I was home before he was. He knew that America had been attacked; teachers had announced it to the older elementary students before a directive came not to discuss it. However, my son was initially feeling more of a bravado about it. The enormity of the devastation hadn't really sunk in to his eleven-year-old mind. He had only heard that planes had smashed into buildings and that America would certainly fight back. Carman didn't know that both of the Twin Towers had imploded and collapsed, and until we sat there together watching the coverage on TV, I don't think he had realized the enormous loss of life and devastation the terrorists had caused.

So we sat there together, my son and I, on a beautiful early fall afternoon, watching the replays on TV of a plane seemingly swallowed into a tall building. We watched fire and smoke mushrooming, people screaming, running, crying, and the towers of New York falling into the ground like decks of cards. It was a much more somber child who sat and saw exactly what had happened to the United States of America played out on his television screen. We watched, we talked, and we prayed for all the victims, their families, and the country we loved.

After several hours of absorbing the news and listening to our president reassure the American people about what he termed was "an act of war" against our country, I decided that we needed a break from the shock of what had happened to our land. "Let's go visit Aunt Jane for awhile," I said. I went into my bedroom to change out of the work clothes I'd had on since early morning, instructing my son to change out of his school clothes as well. I pulled on a pair of jeans and a sweatshirt, brushed my hair, walked out of my room, and then I saw him. My young son, all five feet five inches of him, stood straight and tall in the middle of our living room dressed in his Boy Scout uniform. Tears immediately sprang to my eyes.

"Do you think I should wear this?" he asked me. I looked at my son, and I remembered stories of other Scouts from years ago, Scouts who had bravely ignored the blaring sirens during the blitz of London in World War II and raced out to help rescue people buried in the bombed ruins of buildings. Scouts who harvested food and evacuated children to safer places. I thought of the Scouts who had risked their lives to deliver messages to those working in the Resistance, and I remembered the Scouts who lived in Nazi-occupied countries where Scouting was considered a serious threat and banned. Even under the threat of losing their lives, those Scouts of years ago refused to disband. Boy Scouts furtively exchanged salutes on the street and met secretly in the dark woods under starlit skies, refusing to give in to those who would extinguish their organization. In those dark, war-torn years of horror, boys and girls maintained their faith in their countries and in Scouting, and drew from its ideals and traditions the strength of mind and of purpose to endure.

My thoughts came back to the present, to my young son standing there in his uniform, asking me if I thought he should wear his uniform that night—the night the fabric of America's safety and freedom was rent and torn.

"Yes," I replied. "Yes, I think you should wear it. The Boy Scouts have always helped their country, doing whatever they could and whatever was needed. During wartime the Scouts have always been part of our homeland defense, and I think it will make people feel a little bit safer and a little bit prouder seeing you in uniform."

Carman nodded, then paused before he spoke. "I think I'll wear it to school tomorrow, too," he said. There was a strength in his voice I'd never heard before. My son, like most other young people, was suddenly changed on September 11, 2001. Now at bedtime there would always be a prayer for his country and all its allies, besides the prayers for loved ones he remembered each night. Now Carman saw himself not just as a boy but also as an American citizen. The words of the Boy Scout pledge he recites each week are no longer casual words but a solemn vow.

Out of the ashes and devastation, we have seen America pull together in unity as never before in this generation. I see it in the flags waving on street corners, and especially I see it in the eyes of a young man who stands erect and tall in his uniform, while his voice rings out loudly and clearly: "On my honor, I will do my best to do my duty to God and my country."

A Woman's Journey

The Cliff

by Melanie Bowden,
Davis, California

It is a warm Sunday evening in October. My fiancé, Mark, and I are at my place getting ready to go out to meet with friends in San Francisco. We are going to a club to see a hilarious cabaret singer. We've seen her many times, and it's always a fun evening.

However, I'm not that excited about going out tonight. I'm nervous. My period is over a week late, and I'm sure that my worrying about it is making it even later. This has happened before, and Mark assures me everything is fine. He knows what a worrier I am. He suggests we run over to the drugstore, get a pregnancy test, and take it before we go out. Then we can relax and have a good time.

We get the test and come back to my apartment. After following the directions, I leave the test stick on the bathroom sink because I'm far too anxious to watch the results slowly appear. Mark and I hold hands in the bedroom while we wait the allotted test time. After going in to check the stick, I come out and look at Mark.

"It's a plus sign," I whisper.

Then I sit down on my bed. The shock immobilizes me for hours. My mind scrambles for reasons why this is a mistake. Obviously, we're not going to make it to the club tonight. We don't sleep very well either.

Monday morning arrives. I call in sick and go to my doctor for a real pregnancy test. I keep reminding myself of the inaccuracies of the take-home ones as I sit in the doctor's waiting room. After they administer my test, a nurse comes into the examination room to tell me the results.

"Well, you're pregnant," she calmly says.

I blurt out, "That's impossible! I'm always so careful."

"Honey, unless you practice abstinence, it's not impossible!"

I am numb. Mark and I aren't marrying until the following June, and we weren't planning on having kids for about four years. The remainder of the day is a blur. I hole up in my apartment, calling and confiding in only my closest friends. In my pocket is the abortion clinic number I asked the nurse to give me. Shaking, I dial the number and schedule the procedure for Friday morning. I'm not ready to have a baby, but my insides feel sick about making the appointment.

Tuesday and Wednesday I stumble through work, sure that everyone can tell I'm pregnant even though I can't be more than six weeks. The fact that I'm going in for an abortion Friday never leaves my mind. Mark is incredibly supportive. He leaves the decision completely up to me, but I sense it's not what he wants. I am so scared. Knowing that this is Mark's baby, the man whom I plan to spend the rest of my life with, wrenches my heart. I start fantasizing about what the baby will look like. I wonder if it is a boy or girl. Does the baby look more like Mark or me? I also get very angry. Why did this have to happen now? Why isn't birth control fail-proof? More important, why did I never fully grasp the ramifications of premarital sex?

I continue to agonize over my situation. I wonder

how Mark and I will feel when we have children later while knowing we didn't keep our first. Can I live with that? Can Mark? If I do keep the baby, how will we manage financially and emotionally? I call an old friend whom I know has had an abortion and is now the mother of a five-month-old girl. Her words are chilling.

"You've been given a gift. Don't do what I did. You will always regret it."

That night I lay in bed asking God for guidance. My friend's words play over and over in my mind. Their power is undeniable.

I wake up Thursday morning and know I can't go through with the abortion. I call the clinic to cancel my appointment, and that sick feeling I have been having dissipates. I'm still terrified, but I feel as if I have just pulled back from the precipice of a cliff.

To this day, I shudder about what I almost did, especially when I look in my beautiful daughter's blue eyes that are so much like my husband's. I went to the edge of a cliff. I'm so thankful God helped me make the choice not to jump.

Chapter Five

Life Lessons

I will instruct you and teach you in the way you should go;
I will counsel you and watch over you.

Psalm 32:8

Whether you turn to the right or to the left,
your ears will hear a voice behind you, saying,
"This is the way; walk in it."

Isaiah 30:21

A Woman's Journey

It Isn't the End of the World

by Barbara Jeanne Fisher,
Fremont, Ohio

Reprinted with permission from The Messenger of the Sacred Heart *magazine, Toronto, Canada, June 1995.*

As a little girl, I fell down on the pavement and scraped my knee. Although it was a minor hurt, at such a young age, it seemed major to me. I began to cry, and when I was certain I had my mother's complete attention, I cried even harder. I will never forget how much better it felt when Mama washed my knee and applied medication and a bandage. She kissed my cheek, held me close, and whispered, "Honey, I know how much it hurts, but believe me, it's not the end of the world."

Years later, when I was engaged to be married, my mother tried to encourage me to take time and be certain I had found the right person for a lifetime partner. I was "head over heels in love" and chose to ignore my mother's warnings. After all, what could a mother know about such things? Later, when my significant other turned out to be a real rat, my heart was crushed. I didn't think I could possibly go on living.

Even though she had never approved of the relationship, Mom never said, "I told you so!" Instead, she held me close and let me cry. Then, sharing my sadness as only a mother could, she told me, "I truly know how much you are hurting, but believe it or not, this isn't the end of the world."

She was so right. A year later, I met someone else, and we married a short time later. In the next six years, God blessed us with five beautiful children. I never felt as loved or so happy. Then, just when life seemed almost perfect, I was diagnosed with multiple sclerosis.

Devastated, I was certain my life was over. When Mom came to the hospital to see me, I could see she had been crying. She sat on my bed, and for the longest time, we held each other, unable to talk. There didn't seem to be any right words at such a wrong time. Finally, with tear-filled eyes, Mom took my hand in hers. She repeated those familiar words, "I know this is a terrible, difficult time for all of us to accept. We have to put our trust and life in God's hands, now more than ever. It could be worse, you know. As bad as it seems, it isn't the end of the world."

Indeed it wasn't! For the next twenty-one years, I lived a fulfilling and rewarding life. I watched my five children grow up and now have as many beautiful grandchildren. In spite of my illness, my life has been truly blessed.

Then my mom was diagnosed with Alzheimer's, a disease that can virtually render one senseless. Before she progressed to a state of helplessness, she had temporary periods of normality. During one of those times, Mom asked, "Now, what is this disease I have? What's wrong with my head? Please, please be honest with me."

I tried to tactfully explain her expected prognosis. I felt like a traitor, relating this undesirable life sentence to someone who had always been there for me. My heart was broken. I wanted to run away. Mom listened carefully, grasping my every word. For the longest time, she remained quiet, lost in a world of her own, seemingly so far away. Then suddenly her eyes met mine. Even in the midst of her own private hell, Mom put my feelings first.

"Now, what are you crying for? I'm the one who is sick. You have to be brave enough for both of us. I know how much this hurts you, but regardless of what happens to me, you've got to be strong. In spite of what you think right now, I promise you, this isn't the end of the world."

Mama was right. Her disease progressed rapidly. She reached a point where she no longer was able to hold me close or say all the right things to soothe my pain. She couldn't assure me in troubled times that my world would continue. I missed her gentle encouragement, but I knew that it was my turn to be the strong one. Because she no longer remembered the words, I repeated the prayers she taught me long ago. I listened to her constant meaningless chatter.

Mama still understood kisses, and sometimes I knew that my returning the ones she gave me for so many years to ease my pain somehow helped her. On rare occasions, Mama would smile, but most of the time, she was extremely depressed. Many friends and relatives stopped going to see her because it made them feel uncomfortable. At first this upset me, but then I realized that maybe they never were fortunate enough to have a sweet, gentle lady in their past tell them that no matter how painful or uncomfortable it gets for them, "It truly isn't the end of the world."

Recently as my brother, sister, and I stood in my mother's room shortly after she passed away, we cried and wondered how we would go on without Mom. It was time to say good-bye, and yet none of us would ever be ready for that. We had no choice. Suddenly, peace touched my heart. Somewhere from a faraway place, I could hear my mother whisper, "Cry for the loss that you feel in your heart, but also be happy for me, for I am with God in a place that you can't begin to imagine. Yes, honey, I am gone from your life, but never from your heart. For the last time, I promise you—it isn't the end of your world."

The Wal-Mart Missionary

by Patty Smith Hall,
Hiram, Georgia

"Young lady, would you like a little Bible?" Bill has become somewhat of a fixture at our local Wal-Mart. For as long as anyone can remember, he has sat on the wooden bench right inside the entrance, handing out paper Bibles for anyone willing to take one.

"Son, this here tells you all about the Lord."

Time has caught up with Bill over the past few years. Two heart attacks and a stroke can do that to the human body. Curly black hair now has more salt than pepper in it. His gait, though purposeful, has slowed. Pain shadows his expression when he thinks no one is watching. But his eyes, those mirrors to the soul, still glow like fireflies in a mason jar.

"Here you go, sir."

Over a month's time, Bill hands out thousands of tracts to folks who slow down enough to accept his kind offer. Others pleasantly refuse, but most simply smirk as they hurry out the door. Bill just shakes his head and turns to the next person. And on the fifteenth of every month, he calls a local bookstore and orders more booklets.

"Ma'am, can I give your little girl a Bible?"

I'm not sure why, but Bill has been on my heart lately. It could be that I've noticed the empty bench a lot more lately. Maybe I've missed the little song and dance we always do when he tries to give me a booklet. It never fails; he holds out the two-by-two Book with the sweetest smile on his face. Grinning back, I remind him that I'm a believer and tell him to give it to someone who doesn't know the Lord. And like clockwork, that's how things started today. But the Lord is patient with people like me, and as usual, I felt the urge to talk for awhile. I started with the question that had been burning in the back of my mind since the first time I saw Bill.

"Why?"

I mean, let's face it. Wal-Mart isn't exactly the first place that pops into my head when I think "mission field." My mind goes to Africa or Russia. Someplace far off where the Word of God is oppressed. Even the local battered women's shelter seemed a more appropriate place for spreading the gospel than a discount store. But not to Bill.

The wrinkles around his eyes grew deeper as he glanced over at the crowds gathered around the automatic doors. "Patty, these folks live and die right here in Hiram. Some of them will never see the inside of a church. But they're here, buying groceries or something else. So we need to bring God to them." Bill turned to me, the familiar Book resting in his hand.

Once again, I had put my Lord in a neat little box. Staring at the Book in Bill's outstretched palm, I took it, a gentle reminder from my heavenly Father that His mission field is not a physical place—but a human heart.

The Smiles of Children

by Jennifer Johnson,
Lake City, Minnesota

At age nineteen, I went to southern India to learn about life. To experience, to grow, to change. God gave me the opportunity to do all those things on a three-week field visit I made to a little temple town called Tirupathi. I lived at a small residential school for the children of women who were forced into prostitution at the local temples.

Without this school, the children—especially the girls —would have been left to suffer the same fate as their mothers. I was horrified upon my arrival. The school was located in the middle of an enormous slum, surrounded by poverty, hunger, and sadness. Fear of the unknown overcame me. It lurked everywhere. I did the only two things I could think of. I prayed for strength and healing, and threw myself into the children's daily lives.

I grew attached to those children. I didn't want to leave them when my time was up—a sharp contrast to my initial feelings. At first, I dreaded my stay because I didn't have the "creature comforts" I was used to—running water, a bed, and a bathroom. But my departure date came all too soon. I wanted to stay and somehow watch over those children, to protect them from the cruelties of life, like the poverty that was sure to grip them outside their safe little school.

After we had taken a group picture on my last day, they all swarmed around me, pulling me down into them. I suddenly had a million little hands touching me and a million little mouths kissing my cheeks.

Some of the children had come down with a nasty fever. Little Mamatha was hot and still as she sat on my lap for the longest time that night. Her big brown eyes stared up into mine, telling more than words could have ever explained. I went into the infirmary to say good-bye to Madevi, a girl at the school who was my age. She was sleeping when I crept in to see her. I knelt down on the floor beside her as she rolled over to see me. She opened her eyes and managed a smile through her tears. I smiled back through mine as I grabbed her hand. She kissed my hand and went back to sleep.

Why did those children get dealt such a hard life when my life of privilege was granted to me so easily? I wondered. *I don't deserve my privileges any more than they deserve their constant hardships.*

The most amazing thing about my precious time with them came when I looked into their happy eyes and returned their bright, sunny smiles. I shared their joy, not sadness; their thankfulness for what they had, not their desperate need for money or food; their happiness that they were given this limited opportunity, not their misery at being left behind.

God gave me the chance to experience what I had never known or even dreamed. A chance to understand something completely foreign to me. Through each of those children, God showed me that to fear the unknown, to recoil from the hardships of life, would be to miss out on the greatest gifts He has to share. The simple truth in that lesson has changed my life forever.

Press On!

by Linda LaMar Jewell,
Albuquerque, New Mexico

First published as "Why Fret a Least Favorite Chore?" *in* Why Fret That God Stuff? Learn to Let Go and Let God Take Control. *Compiled by Kathy Collard Miller, published 1998 by Starburst Publishers, Inc.*

Tired and grumpy, I thumped the iron down and closed my eyes. "Oh, Lord, this is boring. My feet hurt. My back hurts. I'm tired of ironing."

When I opened my eyes, the blank wall stared back at me. Sighing, I returned my focus to the collar of a white cotton blouse that soon reflected my rumpled attitude. In my rush to finish my least favorite Saturday afternoon chore, I pressed in some creases while pressing out others.

A few blouses later, I glanced over my shoulder. The summer afternoon was beckoning me. I set the iron down, wandered to the open patio door, and rested my eyes on the patch of green lawn beneath lazy clouds drifting through blue sky.

"God," I exclaimed, "Your creation is more interesting than a blank wall!"

Excited, I raced back to the ironing board and flipped it around so I could face the open patio door instead of the wall.

I now iron in my usual spot, but I've turned my feet and my outlook 180 degrees. Without this change of viewpoint, I would have missed the small delights of watching a butterfly cotillion and chuckling at cheerful robins pirating cherries.

These days, I don't always recall what I've just ironed, but I do remember the changing seasons. Orange and yellow cosmos dance outside the patio door in response to summer's sunlight kisses. Autumn's setting sun is a stained-glass glow through the maroon ornamental crab-apple tree. Quiet winter's snow outlines the garden path, and springtime cheers the progress of a blossom parade.

Intrigued by the bounty of God's beauty, I feel more refreshed after ironing since I've changed my perspective. I look forward to this respite watching the ever-changing seasons. Ironing at a more leisurely pace, I also fabricate fewer new wrinkles.

While my hands are on automatic pilot, my eyes are resting on the scene the Master Gardener creates outside my patio door. I watch God paint my personal, wall-sized Monet—a forever-changing exhibit of His glory.

When we're fretting about our least favorite chores, maybe we just need to change our point of view. We should remember Philippians 4:8, "Whatever is lovely . . .if anything is excellent or praiseworthy—think about such things." God always has a blessing waiting for us. We may just need to turn the ironing board around to see it.

Fruit in Every Season

by Elizabeth Griffin,
Edmonds, Washington

When my friend Kris asked if she could spend the night to break up a ten-hour car trip across the state, I anticipated that a blessing was coming my way. Seeing Kris was always a breath of fresh air to my spirit. What I never expected was that the biggest blessing of this visit would come from Mary, her mother-in-law, who was entering stage two of Alzheimer's.

"I'm sorry. What was I saying? I have Alzheimer's, and I sometimes forget," Mary confessed.

"That must be very difficult," I replied.

"Thank you for understanding," she said with a smile. "Are we in Portland?"

"No," I answered. "We're in Edmonds."

"Oh," she whispered.

As Kris settled her baby for the night in the other room, I was learning about Mary's life as the mother of eight children and wife of an alcoholic husband.

"All my children have done extremely well," Mary said. "Some of them have done so well that they don't want anything to do with me. I think they think I want something from them, but I don't." She sat, momentarily saddened by her memories. Then, brightening, she said,

"You are so kind to have us in your home."

I marveled as I listened to Mary. She had endured a lot of hardship. Now, in her older years, she was struggling with a disease that makes it impossible to control emotions, much less hide any pain or disappointment. And yet, as she told me details of her life, how her husband left and she worked while raising her children, I saw no trace of bitterness. Mary had an air of gracious dignity that only a loving heart could manifest. It was evident that she enjoyed a long and deep relationship with Jesus Christ and learned the secret of having a grace-filled heart. She was one of the most thankful and joyful people I had ever met.

I thought back to the previous two weeks I spent fretting about getting older. My thirty-ninth birthday was just around the corner. Now before me sat a woman whom the psalmist described when he wrote, "The righteous will flourish like a palm tree. . . They will still bear fruit in old age, they will stay fresh and green" (Psalm 92:12, 14).

I expected to minister to this woman who was nearly twice my age, yet it was she who ministered to me. She bore fruit in my life without even knowing it, simply through her heart attitude. She made me hungry for more of God. As I sat opposite Mary in my living room, I found my heart crying out, *Oh, Lord, make me like this! When I am old, and even today, give me the grace to be thankful and not bitter. Make me a fruitful garden.* That night, Mary was God's encouragement to me that He can use us for His glory at every stage of our lives.

The Birthday

by Karen L. Garrison,
Steubenville, Ohio

It was my thirty-fifth birthday—a day I feared like any other maturing person—when I realized my prayers for an "aging revelation" had been given to me. It began with my four-year-old daughter, Abigail, as she bobbed up and down, tugging on my shirt.

"Hurry, Mommy, hurry! Blow out the candles!" she shouted. "And don't forget to make a prayer," she reminded, her brown eyes alight with childish wonder.

"Make a prayer?" her grandmother asked. "What's that?"

"Silly Grammy!" Abigail laughed, covering her mouth. "We say prayers instead of wishes! It's easy!"

The lights dimmed and the candles flickered. Several witty birthday cards on aging were propped beside the cake. Just last month, my older brother refused to celebrate his fortieth birthday. He did not want to be reminded that he was getting older. I closed my eyes and breathed deeply. How many people, including myself, did that each year, becoming less and less thankful for the miracle of their lives?

Remembering Isaiah 40:8, "The grass withers and the flowers fall, but the word of our God stands forever," I asked God to help me stand firm in what He had shown me the previous year during my friend's battle for her life.

My daughter slipped her hand into my pocket—her tiny fingers finding mine. I rubbed her soft skin and sighed, remembering Susie. Mother of two and wife of twenty years, Susie was young and vibrant. She had a welcoming grin, a kind heart. . .and breast cancer. Violently sick from chemotherapy, she lost her hair and began a journey of pain and endurance.

Her husband, desperate for a medical breakthrough, arranged experimental procedures. Nothing worked, and Susie's condition worsened. Time passed, but Susie refused to give up.

Those who knew her best began to doubt her life-and-death decisions. "Why is she doing this to herself?" they'd often asked. "She and her family are going to have to accept the inevitable. She's going to die. She should stop the treatments and live the rest of her days as best she can. Can't she see that?"

I thought I knew the answer. I joined a prayer partner to diligently lift Susie in prayer from the onset of her cancer. Everyone who loved Susie wanted what was best for her. Some chose the "live your remaining days free of medical services" approach. Others continued helping her find new alternatives. Whatever their advice, Susie never wavered from one path—doing whatever she had committed to do in order to beat the disease. She continued medical treatment though her doctors told her there was little hope.

During Susie's struggle, at night when I cradled my newborn son, I often thought of her family who would be left behind if she died. Maybe it was because of how I loved my own children and husband that her battle affected me so greatly.

Looking at life through Susie's eyes filled me. A new humility and appreciation for each day surrounded me.

When my husband kissed me as he left for work, I'd linger in his arms a little longer. Every night, I'd kneel beside my sleeping children and study their angelic faces—not wanting to take one second for granted. Soon, I began to ache for Susie, and during that time I realized why she continued with such passion.

Susie knew the secret of life. And that secret, simply, was life itself.

She wanted another opportunity to laugh and smack her husband's hand as he lovingly pinched her when she walked past. She wanted to witness her daughter's high school graduation and her son's first prom. She wanted to see God's glory in another sunrise and wanted to be in the world when her first grandchild entered it. Life was not a mystery but a miracle. And Susie knew that, right up until the moment, on a crisp winter day, she died.

"Mama," Abigail said, pointing to the candles. "Hurry, they're melting!"

My husband, holding our precious son, Simeon, caught my eyes from across the table. He kissed the top of Simeon's head and smiled at me. Butterflies fluttered in my stomach. Those whom I loved most were near.

Because of Susie's zest for life and faith in God, I've never seen birthdays in the same way. Anxiety didn't flood me at my first wrinkles. And since Susie's death, I've never bought an insulting birthday card. Instead, I've embraced the joys and trials of getting older. After all, each birthday is one more year that I've experienced life's many jewels. Jewels ranging from my children wrestling with my husband to a bird's morning song awakening me.

"Hurry, Mama! Hurry!" Abigail pleaded. "I'll help you blow them out!"

My son giggled, waving his hand at me. My husband

winked. "Let's do it," I told my daughter. We filled our cheeks with air and blew out the candles. The smoke traveled upward.

"Look, Mama! Look!" Abigail shouted, pointing a finger toward the ceiling. "The smoke's carrying your prayer to heaven! It's gonna be answered!"

Bending down, I cupped Abigail's beautiful face. Her eyes beamed, and I inhaled the sweet scent that was hers exclusively. "It already has, honey," I whispered, thanking God for another year. "It already has."

Hope Blooms

by Lynn D. Morrissey,
Ladue, Missouri

January was a bleak month. My husband suffered a heart attack and nearly died, I experienced incredible complications and pain from foot surgery, and I learned that my beloved great-aunt was dying. My hope, like an ugly amaryllis bulb which I'd just planted in a pot on the kitchen windowsill, lay buried beneath ugly fears.

I anguished over Great-aunt Martha's rapidly deteriorating health. Colon cancer ravished her body with unrelenting fury. My husband, Michael, and I visited her daily in a hospice nursing home, watching her once-supple skin shrivel tightly over her angular skeleton. Yet somehow, the greater her pain and weakness, the greater became her determination to live.

Martha had an indomitable spirit, a generous heart, and an inexhaustible capacity for joy. Each day we visited, resigned to her death, but left renewed by her life. Yet, the cancer prevailed.

The closer she came to death, the more I feared for her salvation. My aunt was one of the most kindhearted and gracious of women, but she wasn't a Christian. Whenever I talked about God, she grew uncomfortable. While she never told me to stop, out of respect for her I did. Now, with no time to lose, I prayed whenever I was with Martha. Each time, she literally pushed me away, saying, "Please stop, honey. You're scaring me." We were extremely close, and I knew she wasn't upset with me personally. It was my praying that made her so nervous. Yet, I gently persisted.

Shortly before Martha was transferred to the nursing home, we met a wonderful hospital chaplain named Jim. I shared with him my concern over Martha's salvation, and he agreed to visit Martha regularly to comfort her and share the gospel. Martha looked forward to his visits and "flirted" with him in her impish, mischievous, eighty-two-year-old way. Yet, whenever Jim shared about Christ, Martha grew uneasy. She was especially frightened when he prayed.

Jim, my family, and I continued to pray fervently that God would save Martha, and that He would give us some indication that He had.

One day, before I left the nursing home, I told Martha I was going to pray for her. Once more she pushed me away, expressing her fear. This time, I remained by her bed, strongly sensing God directing me to ask her why she was afraid. After a long pause, she was able to articulate: "I'm afraid of dying."

Finally, she had named the terror that gripped her whenever God's name was mentioned. I realized that she had equated my prayers with my knowledge of her impending death. I was so relieved to share with her that she didn't need to fear the only One who could help her.

"Oh, Martha," I explained, "there is nothing to fear. God loves you so much that He gave His only Son to die for you. He took your place and mine for all the wrong things that we have done. Jesus suffered a horrid death, so He truly understands how terribly you are suffering now. He doesn't want you to hurt anymore and wants to take you to heaven to live with Him forever. All you have to do is to ask Him."

Martha grew sleepy, and I left. I called Jim to tell him all that had happened. A couple days later, Jim visited Martha. As soon as Jim greeted her, though incredibly weak, she countered with, "Oh, no. It's you!"

Jim said she was half joking but likely anticipated that he would talk to her about God. This time as he leaned down by her bed, with all her remaining strength, Martha raised up and hugged his neck with such force that he dropped to his knees.

"I'm so afraid to die," Martha barely whispered in his ear.

Jim assured Martha that there was absolutely nothing to fear, that if she knew Christ when she died, she would instantly be in heaven with Him. Without coaxing or forcing Martha, Jim simply asked if she wanted Jesus to save her. She said, "Yes." Though her words were barely audible, she repeated Jim's prayer.

The next day when I saw Martha, she tried to hug me, but her arms collapsed by her sides. She quietly whispered, "I love you." I sat on her bed for over an hour, stroking her hair and moistening her lips. Before I left, I asked Martha if I could pray with her. She nodded. I held her and prayed, and this time she didn't push me away. She was completely peaceful. She smiled sweetly and radiated incredible joy. I knew that the Holy Spirit now resided in my aunt's heart. I knew that she was ready to die! Ready to live!

When I got home, as I lingered at the kitchen sink, I noticed emerald amaryllis shoots towering over the pot. In the course of less than two months since I'd planted the bulb, I'd watched in amazement at the leaves' sky-rocketing growth. I was eager to see the red blooms promised by the potting instructions.

The next day we got a call from my cousin to say that Martha had died the night before, shortly after Michael and I left her. I felt nothing. I couldn't cry. Daddy and I prepared for the funeral. He wrote a beautiful eulogy. I arranged the music and asked Jim to officiate.

The morning of the funeral, as I filled the teakettle at the sink, amazingly I beheld three bright crimson blossoms. The amaryllis trumpets had bloomed simultaneously, joyously heralding my aunt's going home to heaven. To me, they represented the Father, Son, and Holy Spirit, keeping Their promise to welcome her in love. Suddenly, my tears flowed.

I considered how light and life paradoxically spring from darkness and death, how silver linings peek beneath dark clouds, butterflies flutter forth from cocoons, and amaryllises emerge from clod-covered bulbs.

I realized that although Aunt Martha had endured one of the longest, most excruciating deaths possible, God used her suffering to cause her to reach out to Him for salvation when she might not have otherwise. Her suffering was a momentary, light affliction compared to the eternal joy she was now experiencing in heaven.

Recipe for a Good Cry

(For the Grieving Soul)
by Linda Evans Shepherd,
Longmont, Colorado

From Love's Little Recipes for Life, *Multnomah.*

Cook's Note: Do not hold your tears back in this recipe. The more you use, the better the results.

Ingredients:

> Gush of tears
> Box of tissues
> Five minutes of solitude

Directions:

> We sometimes keep our feelings bottled inside. But in ancient times, women released them in order to capture their tears in tiny keepsake bottles. Tears must be released so that steam will escape our emotional pressure cooker.
>
> For a good cry, go to your bedroom with a box of tissues. Close the door and allow feelings to surface until they overflow, five to thirty minutes per time. If you are experiencing severe pressure, you may need to repeat this process for several days. This will prevent you from having emotional explosions and deep depressions.

Chapter Six

Angels Among Us

Keep on loving each other as brothers.
Do not forget to entertain strangers,
for by so doing some people have entertained angels
without knowing it.

Hebrews 13:1–2

Internet Angels

by Susan Farr Fahncke,
Kaysville, Utah

My sister was twenty-eight years old and dying. Diagnosed with an inoperable brain tumor, Angel would be gone by this summer, we were told. It was April, and the weather outside matched this time in her life. Stormy, winter half over, the promise of spring on the horizon. It was a time of waiting and anguish, a time of learning to live in peace and coming to terms with the end of life as we had known it. Reeling from both physical pain and the pain of her husband simply walking out of her life, my young sister bore loneliness and sorrow of the deepest magnitude. Hard as I tried, I could not erase her sadness. Our days were spent together with me desperately trying to make her smile and forget, if even for a moment, her deep loneliness.

I run a Web site and send out daily inspirational stories. The members of my "on-line family" are an amazing group of people. Many have suffered through a great deal. Through their letters and stories, I have come to love these people. They have survived cancer; divorce; homelessness; the death of a child, a spouse, a parent, a sibling; disabling accidents; heartache; and pain of every other kind. Somehow, life has a way of creating kindness and compassion in the wake of pain.

I found writing about my sister's illness cathartic,

and I shared many of our experiences with my daily list. Through my stories, Angel became a part of the lives of these gentle and loving people. Gifts and cards began to arrive for my sister. Relationships with people all over the world developed. As the tumor grew and my sister's ability to communicate, to walk—to live—deteriorated, hundreds of letters and cards, and most of all, prayers, poured forth. And through it all, as her life slowly seeped away, her spirit began to transform. Being loved can create a miracle.

In the beginning of April, I found an incredible site at www.chemoangels.com. I had no idea that clicking on that link would put my sister's heart back on a path of healing, of love. It opened up a world of kindness that became a rainbow during the last weeks of Angel's life. Daily cards, letters, and packages arrived only two days after I signed Angel up for a "Chemo Angel." She had hundreds of angels who reached out with boundless love and compassion. Between the dear friends Angel made from my Web site family and the Chemo Angels, every day of her life brought surprises of love and friendship. My sister's loneliness began to subside and was replaced with the thousands of strangers—angels—who unconditionally loved her and gave her back her smile.

Each day's mail brought stuffed animals, angels of every size, shape, and type. It brought flower seeds, candles, and inspiring cards that strengthened her faith when she needed it most. Unable to walk to the mailbox, she would eagerly wait until I brought the stacks of love hidden in envelopes—all just for her. Her face, swollen and scarred from the chemotherapy and the many falls she had taken, would at last be filled with light and laughter, a gift from heaven wrapped in the love of strangers.

They didn't know it, but each of these dear people

created a haven of reprieve from pain for my sister. Her bedroom was filled with their gifts, constant reminders that she was indeed loved, and that God does send angels to do His work. These angels had a very short time to perform a miracle, but they accomplished it with the flurry of angels' wings and the sparkle of heavenly dust. They showered love on my sister with such intensity and such zest that her loneliness evaporated in their warmth.

The week before she died, Angel and I made a pact. In her halting words, she told me if I would be a Chemo Angel, she would be a "Guardian Chemo Angel." I had already applied and was an "angel in waiting." She was delighted, her blue eyes lighting up as our pact was sealed with tears and a sister-hug.

The following Monday, April 30, Angel's spirit left her body. I felt the deepest aching pain I had ever known. The next few weeks were filled with numbness and heartache, but then tiny miracles began to appear in my mailbox every day. Cards with little angels on the return address labels poured, like a cooling summer rain. Day after day brought hundreds of cards, many with angel pins tucked inside, the prayers of countless angels prodding me to look for the rainbow.

Six weeks after Angel's death, I received an E-mail that made my heart skip a beat. It was my first Chemo Angel assignment. A grin slowly spread across my face as tears simultaneously poured down my cheeks. I knew that this patient was going to have two angels, not just one. I wanted to find just the right way to introduce myself and let her know she had an angel in her corner. I finally hit on the perfect thing. It was an E-card with a beautiful, serene angel, wings spread wide. At the bottom, "An angel is watching over you" was written in elegant lettering.

Excited, I looked up at the photo of my sister, taken

before she got sick—when her face retained its full beauty and her eyes sparkled with life. I smiled and let the tears flow as I silently told her I was finally keeping our pact. I wrote a brief introductory note and as I clicked "send," I felt the warmth of a hand on my shoulder. I looked behind me. I was alone. I looked up at Angel's photo, and her eyes seemed to twinkle knowingly back at me. The warmth of her hand remained on my shoulder, and I knew that she was with me as we kept our sister-pact to care for someone just as she had been cared for. At last, I could begin to repay the gift that was given Angel during her last weeks on earth. I was grateful to finally be a Chemo Angel, to finally take part in the miracle of giving unconditional love to someone like my sister. At last I was a Chemo Angel, and Angel was a very special guardian angel. "Internet angeling" had come full circle.

Midnight Serenade

by Sandra J. Campbell,
Garden City, Michigan

I slowly descended the stairs, hurting more with each step. "Mike, I think I need to go to the hospital," I whimpered. I had been sick for three weeks and had already been through two rounds of antibiotics. My fever was back up to 104 degrees. The light hurt my eyes. Every part of me ached. I tried to lie down to rest but awoke feeling worse than before. "Something must be wrong. I'm just not getting any better," I lamented.

Mike took one look at me and agreed. Off to the emergency room at St. Mary's Hospital where the doctors poked and prodded, trying to figure out the problem. After five hours of blood tests and X-rays, they decided to admit me. The pain came in waves. First my head pounded, then my eyes blurred, then the fever spiked, and awful pain traveled throughout my body. The doctor had no clue about my condition.

"Must be a virus," he said.

Late that night a woman was admitted to my semi-private room. Obviously in a lot of pain, she must have come up from surgery. She woke me from a fitful sleep. She was hysterically yelling at the nurses.

"Give me pain medication. My doctor told me I would not have any pain. Give me something now!" she screamed.

All I could think was, *Oh, brother! Guess I'm not getting any sleep tonight.* My head started pounding again.

The nurses refused her demands, and then I heard her make a phone call. It must have been to her husband. "Come and get me right now! I want outta here! I have medicine at home if they won't give it to me here. If you won't come and get me, I'll call a cab!" she wailed. She slammed the phone down and yelled some more. This was going to be a long night.

I shuffled into the bathroom, pulling my IV pole with me. *Lord, how can I help this woman?* I prayed. On the way back to my side of the room, I stuck my head behind her curtain and said, "I'm sorry you are in so much pain. Is there anything I can do to help?"

She immediately calmed down and said her doctor had promised her she would not have any pain, but the nurses would not listen to her plea for medicine. I told her I was a Christian and asked if I could have a word of prayer with her. I motioned to the crucifix on the wall and gently reminded her that Jesus knew all about pain and suffering.

I held her hand and prayed, "Lord, we thank You that You are the Great Physician. Thank You that You care about our suffering. Thank You that You were willing to suffer for us by dying on the cross in our place. You know just what we are going through right now. I ask You to please comfort this dear lady, ease her pain, and help us praise Your name even now in this place. In Jesus' name, amen."

She thanked me for such a sweet prayer and told me that she, too, was a believer. The Holy Spirit gave me the courage to proceed by asking her if she had heard of a song called "Promises." Would she mind if I sang it for her right now? "Please do," she said.

A Woman's Journey

Normally, I am terribly shy. When I sing with the ladies' trio at church, I stand in the middle so they can hold me up if I start to crumple! Never would I have dreamed to offer a solo. But, here I was, at midnight, singing a cappella in a darkened hospital room! I don't remember who wrote the song, but I softly sang it to her.

My voice trembled and cracked out the song I learned so long ago. Somewhere between my feeble attempt and my roommate's two ears, God changed that song into a beautiful melody that encouraged her heart. She was blessed and asked, "Could you please sing it again? That was just beautiful!" she exclaimed. I timidly complied.

Then I had an idea. "Do you know any praise choruses?" I asked.

"A few," she replied.

"Why don't we sing them together?" I suggested.

There we were. Strangers, yet sisters in the Lord. We softly sang together sweet songs of faith, and we were blessed. I remembered the story in Acts 16:25–26 about Paul and Silas and how they sang and prayed at midnight, their chains fell off, and God delivered them from prison. Then I thought about how we sang and praised God for His goodness to us, and our chains of pain and discouragement were broken, and our spirits were set free to worship our Lord.

After an hour or so I bade her good night, and we slept soundly the rest of the night. I heard her talking on the phone the next morning with friends and noticed that her whole attitude had changed. Later that day, her husband came to take her home. She was in such a sweet frame of mind that he asked what had come over her. She told him, "The Lord sent an angel to pray and sing with me last night."

Now that's the first time anyone other than my

husband has called me an angel! I do know as I yielded myself to the Lord that He answered my prayer for help. He gave me clear direction and the boldness I needed to be a blessing to a stranger. Together we sang psalms, hymns, and spiritual songs, making melody in our hearts to the Lord.

My New York Angel

by Allison Gappa Bottke,
Faribault, Minnesota

Even though I was only fourteen, I was an "old" fourteen, if you know what I mean. A strong-willed child raised by a single, working mother, life dealt me a hand of cards that forced me to grow up fast. Plus, full-figured and five feet seven, I always passed for someone years older. And so, when my mother threatened to send me away if I continued to see my eighteen-year-old boyfriend, Jerry,* I took matters in my own hands. I ran away from home.

"There's no way she's going to keep us apart," Jerry said as he handed me the money to buy my airplane ticket and $200 to tide me over until I found a job. "I made a reservation for you to leave tomorrow. Pretend you're sick in the morning and don't go to school, pack a bag, and get out before she gets home. You can take a taxi to the airport. Here's the phone number of my friends in New York. They'll put you up for awhile. Call them as soon as you land."

I clutched my suitcase as I ran through the airport to catch my plane, hoping that I hadn't forgotten anything important in my rush to leave home before Mom got back from work.

This will show her how serious we are, I thought victoriously. This was my first plane ride and my first love.

The thought of being forbidden to see him was unbearable. The thought of being a fourteen-year-old girl alone in New York City didn't bother me.

Landing at LaGuardia Airport at eight o'clock on a Saturday night was the beginning of a journey that would change my life. A journey where, quite simply, the Lord sent me a New York angel whose unconditional love saved my life.

Walking excitedly to the pay phone to call Jerry's friends, I thought about this luxurious, newfound freedom. I would find a job, and in a few weeks Jerry would join me. We'd marry and live happily ever after.

Ah, the sweet ignorance of youth! As the phone rang, I dreamed of married life, of the idyllic way everything would turn out. Mom would see how wrong she was, and one day we'd all laugh about this.

"The number you have reached is not a working number. . . ." I jumped at the sound of the recording. *I must have dialed wrong,* I thought. Trying again, this time more carefully, I began to feel a frightening apprehension creep through my body. Shaking it off, I assured myself that everything would be fine.

"The number you have reached. . ." It was true. The number was disconnected. I hung up the phone and stood very still.

There was no way I could reach Jerry that night as he had rented a room without a phone, and I wasn't about to call home. "Okay," I said to myself. "This isn't the end of the world. Find a hotel or a YWCA until you can reach Jerry at work in the morning."

I forced myself to look on the bright side as the alternative would have crippled me. Just think, here I was in New York! The Big Apple! And, since it was 1970, the first thing I thought about was Greenwich

Village. The city of peace, love, and flower power! I'd find somewhere in the Village where I could stay the night. It mattered little to me that it was getting late and that I all but reeked of "vulnerable underage runaway."

When I arrived, the Village was aglow in lights, a street festival was underway, and artists lined the corridor. Singers, street dancers, and vendors were everywhere, just like on television. After the taxi, phone calls, subway, and the snack I had at the airport, I still had about $150, a lot of money (or so I thought) in those days. *Certainly, it will be more than enough to last me for weeks,* I ignorantly thought. I stopped at a hotel and was told it was fifty dollars for the night. "How could they?" I gasped. Were hotels really that expensive? Fear began to grip my heart, but I fought it with all my might.

By 11:00 P.M., the street vendors were beginning to close up shop. Artists were packing up, and the gay feeling of people hustling and bustling was replaced by another kind of atmosphere. Women in short dresses— very short dresses—began to appear. Men with lots of jewelry and fancy cars lined the streets. People passed bottles and strange-smelling cigarettes among themselves, and I began to notice large cardboard boxes off the beaten path, boxes that on closer inspection seemed to be—could it be. . .houses? Did people actually live on the street? I held tightly to my suitcase and continued to walk, repeating over and over to myself that everything would be fine.

Then I saw her work. Canvas touched by God. Paintings and pencil sketch drawings hung on the fence, the content of which called out to me. While I was growing up, Mom often took my siblings and me to the art museum. I knew what it was like to be moved by art. My heart raced.

"Can I help you?" I looked up to the round, pleasant face of a woman who looked to be my mom's age, a woman whose kindness made her glow.

"Did you draw these?" I asked in awe.

"Do you like them?" she responded.

"I love them! Oh, how I'd love to have talent like that," I exclaimed.

"Everyone has some special talent, my dear. One day you'll find yours," she said. "My name is Tanya. What's yours?"

I can't recall what we talked about next, but eventually I asked if she knew where I might find a YWCA. At that question, she looked me straight in the eye and without hesitation said, "Please, come home for the evening with my daughter, Claudette, and me. We have plenty of room. This city is a difficult place to get around in during the daytime, let alone in the evening. You can get a room tomorrow."

I wasn't in the habit of going anywhere with strangers, let alone to someone's home to sleep. But then again, I wasn't in the habit of running away from home either. I accepted her offer.

I shudder to think what may have happened to me had I not. There is no doubt in my mind had I remained on the dark and dangerous streets of New York City, I would have become another runaway statistic. "Then no harm will befall you, no disaster will come near your tent. For he will command his angels concerning you to guard you in all your ways" (Psalm 91:10–11). The Lord sent my angel. Her name was Tanya Cervone.

The next day I called the warehouse where Jerry worked, only to find out he had been fired several days earlier. Calling my best friend, I learned the police were looking for me, and when they found me I would be sent to Juvenile Hall. My fairy tale turned into a night-mare. My world was falling apart, but I was determined to hang on. Determined no one would know how frightened I was.

I found a YWCA in the phone book and planned to check in and immediately hit the streets to find a job. Having watched the Macy's New Year's parade every year, I thought I'd start there. I'd go to Macy's and get a job as a salesclerk. I thanked Tanya for her hospitality and asked for directions. Unbeknownst to me, Tanya had listened in on my frantic phone calls. I was certain my story of graduating from high school was totally convincing. It didn't dawn on me that she knew from the start I was a runaway.

"Please stay until you find a job," she said. "I'm sure you'll find something in no time, and then you can get a little apartment. Those rooms at the 'Y' are so small and dingy."

I had to admit the comfort of Tanya's apartment would definitely be better, not to mention safer, and it would allow me to save some money, so I accepted. I put on the only dress I brought and asked for directions to Macy's. On my way, I felt certain everything would be okay, even though a sick feeling developed in the pit of my stomach.

Years later, I found out that while I was gone that first day, Tanya went through my things, located my mom's name and phone number, and contacted her in Ohio. Tanya assured Mom that I was okay and that if the police were called, it might get me home but wouldn't keep me there. "She has to go home on her own; otherwise, you'll only lose her again," Tanya told my mom. "Trust me; I think maybe I can reach her."

During the next few days, I was repeatedly turned

down for jobs because I didn't have acceptable identification. I grew more and more confused and frightened. Finally reaching Jerry, it was of little comfort when he called me a crybaby and said that if I really loved him I'd "get it together and get enough money" to help him come out to join me since he had given me all of his available cash. "Do whatever you have to do," he hissed at me over the phone. "You're in New York City; with your looks and body you could make a fortune out there. Figure something out soon. I've gotta get out of here, and you owe me," he said, hanging up on me.

Unable to stand the fear any longer, I tearfully confided in Tanya. Never before had I shared such intimate feelings with an adult and been so totally accepted. Mom tried hard to be a good parent, but feelings were not something easily shared or discussed in my house. With Tanya it was different. She spoke of what it was like as an artist, what it was like to create these paintings from her mind's eye. She talked of her life in another country and her own trials and tribulations, and she encouraged me to talk about mine. She asked me serious questions, personal questions, and she really listened to my responses. It was as though a dam had burst. We talked for hours. I never knew that kind of communication existed. I went home a few days later of my own free will.

I could have been a thief (or much worse), yet she took me in. I could have made her life miserable, yet she gave me the heavenly protection of her heart and home, unconditionally. I never saw Tanya again, yet our Christmas cards and letters were as consistent as the seasons until she passed away a few years ago.

When I learned of her death, I cried first, then smiled at her memory. She reached out and protected a vulnerable, frightened teenager, giving me peace, refuge, and love. She exhibited the love of Christ in the truest and purest form.

Thank you, Tanya, for being my New York angel. . . . Thank You, Lord, for the gift of her unconditional love.

* name changed

Treasure Hunting

by Cheryl Norwood,
Canton, Georgia

"Come on over tomorrow. All the children have gone through Granny's things, and now it's time for the grandkids to come and get what they want."

My uncle had been put in charge of disposing of my grandmother's things since she lived with him the last few years of her life. Granny died from congestive heart failure but had been suffering from Alzheimer's for the past few years. In a way, we lost her months before her tired heart gave up and she went home to be with Jesus. Knowing she was no longer confused and scared but in the peaceful presence of God gave us comfort. Still, we missed her.

Granny had been a mother to seven, grandmother to more than twenty, and I can't even begin to count the great- and great-great-grandkids. We are a diverse bunch, my family. My cousins and I range in ages from eighteen to forty-six. We represent just about every lifestyle out there—from rural country folk to urban yuppies. Managers and executives to blue-collar factory workers. Health-care professionals to secretaries.

Our only common denominator, the glue that kept us connected, was Granny. She loved the biggest rascal and scoundrel among us just as much as the one climbing the corporate ladder. She made us all feel like we were the favorite! She could make us smile and talk and forget our differences and resentments. We'd do anything to see that twinkle in her eye and that face-splitting grin of hers. We counted on her unconditional love. When no one else cared, when no one else wanted us, we knew Granny did.

Granny never preached to us. Her unconditional love spoke volumes about God's unconditional love. In her own quiet way, Granny was our John the Baptist. I suddenly wanted more than anything to find something of hers that would keep her in my heart.

"All right. Is one o'clock okay with you?" I asked my uncle.

"Sure. See you then," he said as he hung up.

Soon I was down in the basement apartment where she had lived, surrounded by boxes and tables piled with her belongings. I wandered from pile to pile, feeling compelled to touch everything, as if somehow I could connect to Granny through the platter she had piled high with biscuits; the pressure cooker she canned with; the blankets from her bed. Had I ever noticed that she liked figurines of little pigs? Was it being a seamstress that had given her such a love of scissors?

As I opened her closet door, I realized that this was where I got my love of bright colors; every color imaginable jumped out at me from her wardrobe. Red, purple, bright blue. There was the dress she wore to church the weekend she stayed with us. Here was the housedress she liked so much.

On one table were all her treasures, the gifts she had been given over the years. These included mementos and travel trinkets. Although Granny never wandered far from home, her children and grandchildren traveled all over the country—some, even internationally. Granny had traveled through us, been with us in spirit wherever we went. Her prayers followed us everywhere, whether to college or to war.

I was amazed at how much compassion and understanding she had had for so many of her children and grandchildren who had strayed so far from God's best for them. She had been such a good woman herself. Surely God had made her heart, because she loved her lost ones as much as Jesus did. I believe she would have done anything to see some of us not take the paths we had taken. I know she rejoiced when we turned back to God. Either way, she loved us. Even at the end, when she could not put a name to a face, she loved us.

One of my cousins visited her a few weeks before she passed and asked Granny, "Do you know who I am?"

"I can't say your name, but I know I love you," Granny replied.

It was this love that made it so hard to decide what I wanted. There were so many precious items. I wanted to find things that reflected the intangible gifts Granny had given me.

I chose a glass oil lamp. Granny came from humble beginnings, and this lamp had not been bought for decoration. It served a purpose. Granny lived quite a few years without amenities yet had always managed to be joyful. She was a light to her family; this lamp would help me to shine God's light in the lives around me.

I took an old iron, the kind you heat up on the stove. Granny worked hard all her life, without a lot of the advantages and luxuries we enjoy today. Yet she did everything she could for her family. She cooked, sewed, and worked. I think about her hands grasped around the handle of that iron, and the prayers she said for her family as she pressed their clothes and linens. The iron would remind me to keep prayer an everyday part of my life.

Next, there was a pearl-beaded purse with two rows of rhinestones. This one surprised me. Having always known my grandmother as a white-haired, humble woman, this purse reminded me that once upon a time, my grandmother had been young. She had gone to parties; she had danced. She had fallen in love and giggled and agonized over which dress to wear. This purse may have been the finest thing she ever owned. She kept it to remember to stay young at heart and full of dreams. I shall keep it to remind myself that everyone I meet was once young and still has dreams. It will also remind me to keep dreaming myself!

Lastly, I took a little ceramic pitcher from Yellowstone Park. I don't know who gave it to her; I don't really care. It reminds me that all of us were her world. She lived through us and now she lives in us.

No matter where we go, no matter how far, she will always be there. She lives in my love of bright colors; she dances in my uncle's great sense of humor. Her spunk and spirit thrive in Aunt Alice. Uncle Danny and Uncle Alvin look at the world through her soft brown eyes. In each of us, there is a part of her. The same Jesus who lived in her heart lives in ours today. One day we all will be together again. These little earthly treasures remind us of that most important promise, and for that I am forever thankful.

Chapter Seven

Love One Another

*Dear children, let us not love with words or tongue
but with actions and in truth.*

1 John 3:18

Love Thy Neighbor

by Rusty Fischer,
Orlando, Florida

When I finally got home from work that night, I wasn't too surprised to see the door unlocked. My wife had stayed home from work complaining of an upset stomach. I had called home during the day and gotten the answering machine each time. I hadn't been too concerned since she had mentioned a trip to the walk-in clinic to see if they could give her something to help.

All that changed when I saw the broom lying in the middle of the floor. My wife was a confirmed neat freak. It was totally unlike her to leave a broom lying in the middle of the floor. Calling out her name, I noticed other things out of kilter as well. The coffee machine was still on, with strong-smelling black coffee still inside. I switched it off with a shaking hand. Her purse was on the kitchen table, her keys nearby.

I called her name loudly, insistently, as I ran through our two-bedroom apartment, stopping at our bathroom. Plastic wrappers littered the floor with strange symbols and fancy medical terminology covering them. Measurements. Liters. Saline. It looked like something out of an *ER* episode.

Just then a knock sounded at the door and I opened it without hesitation. I was shocked to see that it was our upstairs neighbor. "What do you want?" I asked flippantly of the scraggly college girl who caused us so much grief. Her revolving boyfriends and their big clomping feet, her loud music and late-night parties were the source of many sleepless nights for my wife and me.

Although my wife was always quick to point out that "we'd been young once, too" and how hard it was for a single girl to live alone these days, I'd known that some girls were just plain born bad. My wife would frown. "God doesn't allow His children to be born bad," she'd say sternly. "He doesn't do that. Something made her that way. It's up to us to understand her, help her, and be patient with her. Every one of God's children has a purpose; so does she."

All I ever saw, though, was a noisy brat who kept us up late at night. She was the first person I'd thought of when I saw the broom in the middle of the floor that afternoon. It was the same broom I used to knock on the ceiling at 2:00 A.M. to get her to quiet down!

"Don't you want to know where your wife is?" she asked incredulously. The plot of a true-crime, murder mystery shot through my mind. Had all of my complaints to the apartment complex management finally gotten to this scrawny girl who favored rap albums with thumping bass? Had she taken my griping personally and hired one of her many, questionable boyfriends to kidnap my wife and thus silence the constant complaints? Had my good-hearted and patient wife simply gone up with yet another peace offering in the form of a cake, not to mention a little friendly "witnessing," once too often and happened upon a drug bust gone bad?

I almost said: "What have you done with her?" Instead I simply waited for an explanation.

"I'll explain while you drive to the hospital," she said instead. They were the last words I ever expected to hear from her mouth.

"I woke up late," she said shyly as I drove through town, gritting my teeth at slow drivers and grunting audibly at stoplights that always seemed to see me coming. "I did some laundry, straightened up, and then turned on the stereo real loud."

"Big surprise," I scoffed, hunched over the wheel.

"Well," she said in defense, "I knew you two yuppies would be at your nine-to-five jobs, so I was very surprised to hear thumping underneath me. I looked out the window and, sure enough, your wife's car was still in the parking lot."

"How did you know my wife's car?" I asked, still slightly suspicious.

"I ran into her one day not long after you'd first moved in," she explained, pointing out the way to the hospital. "She asked directions to the mailbox and lent me five dollars," she added sheepishly as I sighed aloud. "Anyway, I figured she was taking the day off so I turned down the music. The thumping kept right on going, quiet and all, but I could tell that's what it was. Finally I turned the music off altogether, but the thumping just kept right on going. I have to tell you, I got a little peeved. So I stomped downstairs to knock on the door. You know, just to ask your wife what her problem was. I knocked and knocked, but no one answered.

"That freaked me out a little," she admitted. "I knew she'd been knocking on the ceiling, and now she wasn't answering? I knew she wasn't afraid of me, having been up to my place so many times with a pound cake or plate of cookies. So I walked over to the rental office and asked them to check on her.

"I followed the manager lady in, and thank God we did. She was passed out on the bathroom floor. There was blood everywhere. I just—"

"Blood?" I shouted, screeching into the huge hospital parking lot. "She had a stomachache this morning and—"

"She'd been throwing up all morning," explained the girl. "Something she ate, I guess. Then, when there was nothing left to throw up, she just kept retching. She ruptured a blood vessel in her throat or something and had started bleeding. It looked a lot worse than it was, but they wanted to take her to the hospital to get her rehydrated and take some electrolyte tests."

The emergency room was crowded, and we sat in silence until a young doctor escorted us back to see my wife. Seeing her in a hospital bed, surrounded by IV tubes and beeping machines as they monitored her rehydration and blood pressure tore into my heart just as fear clawed at my stomach.

What if this skinny, noisy, rap fan upstairs hadn't been home? What if she'd simply ignored my wife's thumping and gone out shopping to the mall for the afternoon? What if my wife hadn't lent her that five dollars, so that this forgetful young girl would always remember her car?

What if I'd been as believing and trusting as my wife?

My wife's eyes flickered in recognition, and a warm smile crossed her pale face. The instinct to run to her and shelter her in my arms was so strong that I nearly leapt across the room. I had not been her protector that day, though. I had been off in my little office with my little job, too caught up in my own troubles to think twice about her "tummy" ache. A problem that no doubt was caused by the questionable all-you-can-eat seafood buffet from the night before.

No, it was our young neighbor who'd been her hero on this day. Despite my protective, loving urges, I stepped aside while at the same time gently prodding the young girl forward. She looked at me hesitantly, and when I nodded, she sprang forward to hug the older, "yuppie" woman with whom she'd so quickly bonded.

As I watched the two women hug, I realized that I was finally witnessing the very embodiment of faith. And I thanked God for a wife who lived first to do His will. . . loving her neighbor as herself. . .in spite of my actions. Where I had always seen a scruffy, scrappy, noisy teenager, my wife had always seen one of God's children. A human being. A person. Perhaps, even, a friend. Now I was seeing the results of a friendship, a friendship that in all probability had saved my wife's life, and it brought tears to my eyes.

Sweet Surrender

by Delores Christian Liesner,
Racine, Wisconsin

As the door swung open, I was shocked. I hardly recognized my friend and coworker, Patti. Her bald head and face were swollen from medication. The only hair the brain surgery and chemotherapy had left was a limp rooster-comb patch that drooped above her forehead.

Had it only been a few weeks since she had experienced those few but alarming lapses in memory? A coworker suggested she have it checked out, and all of us who knew her collectively held our breath when she called only hours later with the diagnosis of malignant brain tumors.

Surgery quickly followed. When Patti called work with an update of her condition, she sent a message with a coworker to tell me that her vision was impaired. She hoped I would know where to get her a large-print Bible. A silent wonder filled me as I thought about the large-print Bible my friend Irene had teasingly offered me the previous month. "You never know when you will need this."

Shortly after that, another message came requesting I call Patti. I was awed to hear her say, "I heard you know what I am looking for. Would you come to see me?"

Honored, yet fearful, I prayed frantically during the forty-five-minute drive to her home. Haunting memories

145

of walking up to the funeral home after my father died and thinking *So this is grief* filled my mind with doubt. How could I help someone through a valley I'd never been through and didn't even like to think about? Someone told her I knew something. . . . *Not something,* my heart cried out. *Someone!* Electrified, I remembered the peace I'd known as God's Word had replaced the fears and doubts so many times in the past. How could I have forgotten! Surrendering, I walked up to her door and stood before Patti.

Her blue eyes gleamed in recognition. Her familiar voice echoed from within a distorted body that even she no longer recognized. She struggled to hand me the huge maroon large-print Bible and simply said, "Show me."

Only three verses came to mind as I silently prayed to meet her need. As she slowly read from John 5:24 and touched the two words "not be condemned," she let out a gasp of delight, tossing me a radiant smile. In my trance of empathy, I was about to go on to the next verse when her other hand wrapped itself around my wrist as she cried excitedly, "Wait! Get a highlighter!"

Surprised, I rose to the table she indicated and returned to her with the yellow marker, watching her carefully mark the words for later reference. "Okay," she said like an eager child. "I'm ready now for the next one." Her voice raised in excitement with each word of 1 John 5:11–13, which stated that "I write these things. . . that you may know that you have eternal life."

She held the edge of her chair excitedly, as if she would leap off and dance. "I can know, I can know," she chanted. "I don't have to wonder or hope anymore. I can know." Again, reminding me of her short-term memory loss, we got the highlighter and she read the verse again as she marked it. This time she put her name in place of the word "you." Her face glowed with joy. We harmonized in happy laughter.

Finally, we looked in the first chapter of Ephesians, which talks about all that we have and are in Christ. Our tears mingled as we hugged and talked about the goals she wanted to reach before she died. We discussed ways she could accomplish them. Her joy seemed limitless and gave wings to my feet as I headed home, humbled and awed by the experience. Her excitement and reactions to verses and concepts I had known for years replayed in my mind and lifted my heart.

We had several more wonderful visits before she died. She laughed. Although she often did not remember what she'd eaten for dinner, or who had visited her that day, she remembered those verses. It's more important, she assured me, to remember the big things: God, her family, and her friends loved her. She looked so forward to seeing Jesus and continually referred to part of a song called, "If You Could See Me Now."

"If you could see me now, you'd know I've seen His face. If you could see me now, the pain is erased. You wouldn't want me to ever leave this perfect place if you could only see me now."

Sometimes I wonder what she had heard that made her call me. It humbles me to know that others are watching and listening even when we are not aware. I wonder if God told her that it was I who needed help and only she could give it. For though she asked me to come give her comfort, I realized that in her joy I had also been given a gift. That was the day I lost the fear of death. I think she knows.

Wisdom and Wrinkles

by Karen O'Connor,
San Diego, California

Previously published in Basket of Blessings *by Karen O'Connor under the title* "Accepting Opportunities," *Waterbrook Press.*

"Karen, I'm calling to let you know that Cliff died the day after Christmas." My heart pounded at the sound of my friend Glenda's voice on my answering machine.

My husband and I had just returned from a glorious trip to Mexico, and this shocking news startled me back to reality. Cliff had died suddenly of heart failure, leaving his wife, their two children, and two teenagers from his previous marriage.

I couldn't get my mind off little Sarah, eight, and Brian, six. Their daddy was gone. In addition, their maternal grandmother had died just two months before, and their paternal grandparents had died days apart two years prior to that. Their maternal grandfather was terminally ill; so he couldn't be present in their lives, and their only uncle and his family lived in Alaska—thousands of miles away. Sarah and Brian had experienced so much loss so early in their lives; I could hardly take it in.

The following Sunday, my husband and I invited

Glenda and the children to brunch after church so we could talk and reminisce and comfort one another. While seated at the restaurant, Sarah seemed listless and disinterested in talking or eating. Brian picked at his food and clung to his mother as we talked.

Suddenly a thought came to me. I leaned over to Sarah and asked if I could rub her back. "When we're sad," I said, "sometimes it helps to have someone who loves us touch us or hold us close."

She moved a little but didn't say anything, so I gently massaged her back and stroked her long hair. Within moments, she sat up and snuggled close to me. My eyes filled with tears. "Since you don't have a living grandma," I said, "I'm wondering if you'd like to adopt me! I have gray hair and wrinkles and ten grandchildren, so I qualify, don't you think? And I sure do love you."

That did it. Sarah nodded her head yes, then drew closer. A moment later she straightened up and smiled. "Would you like to stop by our house and see the goldfish my dad gave me for Christmas?" she asked.

"I'd be happy to," I said. "I'm glad you asked."

We went back to the house, looked at the fish, and played a game. Then as I moved toward the door after saying good-bye, she called after me with joy in her voice: "Bye, Grandma. I love you!"

While walking home I thought, *Lord, what have I done? I'm afraid I acted out of compassion in the moment, but I don't know if I can keep this commitment. We already have so many grandkids of our own.*

Then ever so gently I sensed the Holy Spirit impressing on me that God had assigned me this special job and that He would give me all the resources I needed to do it.

God has been faithful, continuing the good work He

began. It has been four years since that incident and I have never once felt a lack of love or lacked the necessary grace to keep my commitment as Grandma Karen.

Chapter Eight

Hope and Healing

Let us hold unswervingly to the hope we profess,
for he who promised is faithful.

Hebrews 10:23

The Sewing Machine

by Brandi Lentz,
Renton, Washington

Mom and I finally had become friends when her doctor diagnosed lung cancer. The next two years consumed our family as the day we would have to say good-bye neared. I had no idea it would lead me to God.

No matter how much I wished it were someone else's nightmare, I knew I had to prepare my soul for the inevitable. I shook my head at God in wonder. Why did it have to turn out this way? Why did I have to learn how to be the parent when I was just learning how to let my mother parent me?

The last normal conversation I had with my mom was on a Saturday afternoon in August 1994. I had received a sewing machine as a gift. At a different time in my mother's life, she had been a fantastic seamstress. Teaching me to sew was one way she could be my friend and mentor. We had a wonderful conversation that day while making a pair of shorts.

A couple of days later, she suffered a massive stroke. She no longer knew any of us and was unaware of what was happening to her. She couldn't walk, talk, or feed herself. Then her husband was brought into the hospital emergency room. He passed away from a heart attack while Mom was on the fourth floor in the Head Trauma Unit.

Because of Mom's condition, the hospital psychologist advised us against telling her for a few days. When we did tell her, I wasn't sure she understood. On the day of the funeral, I sat with her in the front row. I never will know how much grief she felt.

My mother never came back to me. I never heard her call me by my name again. Her ability to coordinate thoughts with words was gone. She struggled to tell me what she wanted to eat for dinner. Eventually, she gained enough strength to walk and feed herself again, but she could not live alone. With her husband gone, the family decided she would move in with my family and me.

I spent the last week of my mother's life with her in a hospital room. I sat in the chair and watched her labor to breathe. Hospice intervened only to administer pain medication. Family members and friends came to pay their respects and offer condolences.

Sometime during that last week I picked up a Gideon Bible that the hospital supplies to every room. It was the only thing to read. I was a "baby" Christian. I had not yet developed my spirituality, but I was asking all the right questions, seeking answers that I have since found. I didn't know anything about Scripture or the Bible, but I did know that in that Book was comfort.

I opened it and began reading the Twenty-third Psalm aloud. I read because it felt good to me, but it also seemed comforting to my mother. I read another psalm that was just as comforting. I read and reread both psalms. Something compelled me to do this. I did not want to stop.

My mother's breathing eased a bit. She wasn't struggling as much to get the air into her lungs. As I sat there reading, a calm descended upon the room. I knew I was experiencing a miracle. Mom called out to me to "slow down." She wanted to hear the words I was saying. I knew she could feel it, too.

My mother died the next morning at 8:40. I watched as she took her last breath and found peace at last. I know that she is in heaven and that Jesus Christ met her that day to show the way. I know that God was in that room while I was reading His Word to her for the first time in my life. I know today that God is with me always, guiding me during times of struggle.

This event was a benchmark in my Christianity. I reaffirmed my salvation shortly afterward to become a born-again Christian. Each year before the anniversary of my mother's death, I reflect upon the events that took place. Where I used to wonder why, I no longer question. I don't look back with regret that I never got to finish that sewing lesson with Mom. I know it was only a stepping-stone to a different relationship. Although my mother isn't here where I can touch her, she is in a place of peace where I can still read to her.

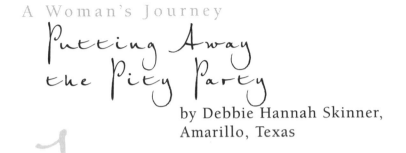

Putting Away the Pity Party

by Debbie Hannah Skinner,
Amarillo, Texas

I was so disappointed with God. Two years after my husband was caught in a "corporate downsizing," our family moved to the Dallas area for his new job. It seemed that everything in my life had changed for the worse. My job as a teacher, once a voluntary joy, was now a demanded drudgery. Our finances were tighter than they had ever been in our twelve-year marriage. My God-inspired dream to work from home on several creative projects was dashed. To make matters worse, there was no hope for change on the horizon.

As I grew increasingly bitter and angry about my circumstances, I drew on my training as a home economics teacher and started throwing a party. This was not your typical social event. It was a pity party.

As I look back at those dark days, it was as though I was carrying around my own invisible Portable Pity Party Pack. It did not contain traditional party supplies of plates, napkins, and cups. It did, however, come with a script that helped me turn every conversation toward my unfortunate circumstances. It led me to overuse words like "if only" and "things were so much better when. . ."

The Portable Pity Party Pack needed a warning label:

"Use at your own risk. Some people will begin to avoid you when you approach them carrying this pack." Nevertheless, I never left home without it. I took it to church. I carried it into my classroom. It was my constant companion.

At the peak of my pity party, we received a phone call from my in-laws telling us that Nanna and Granddad, my husband's grandparents in Missouri, needed some encouragement. Granddad's health was quickly deteriorating, and Nanna's blood pressure was skyrocketing as she went to care for him every day in the nursing home. We had a three-day weekend approaching so we called Nanna to tell her we were coming to visit, hoping to provide some encouragement and much-needed relief from her daily routine. She welcomed us.

That weekend, my husband and daughter went to the nursing home to be with Granddad while Nanna and I stayed at her house. We had a nice visit that day, but as always, I had my Portable Pity Party Pack with me. Nanna sat in her recliner and did not make any comments about my steady stream of complaints. Instead, she listened quietly as I discharged my discontent and disillusionment with God.

The morning we were leaving to return home, Nanna treated us to breakfast before we hit the road. She took us to the best spot in town, the local truck stop. As we went in the door, she carefully slipped a piece of paper in my hand. When we sat down, I discreetly looked at it, trying to hide it in my lap beneath the edge of the plastic tablecloth. On the outside, the name of some drug company was printed. (Granddad had been the local doctor in their small town and had accumulated countless pens and notepads from pharmaceutical companies.)

At first, I thought Nanna was trying to tell me I

needed an antidepressant or something, but when I unfolded the paper and looked inside, I could immediately see the purpose of the note. Nanna had written, "Be joyful always; pray continually; give thanks in all circumstances, for this is God's will for you in Christ Jesus." It was straight out of 1 Thessalonians 5:16–18.

Nanna was not the doctor in her family, but she gave me a prescription for the bitterness that was ailing me. She had listened to me spew my sorrows while saying nothing about the sad circumstance she was in, watching the health of the man she'd loved for more than fifty years deteriorate before her eyes each day. She knew what it meant to suffer loss. But from her years of reading the Bible, she also knew exactly what I needed to be reminded of to make it through my current circumstances. She could see through my pity party and gave me the powerful pieces of God's Word that sustained her and to which I needed to cling.

As we made our way back toward home, those precious words, "For this is God's will for you in Christ Jesus," resounded in my heart. I had been so busy bitterly fighting my circumstances that I stopped being thankful to God for the countless blessings He had given me. It was as though He whispered through those verses, "Debbie, it's time to put away the pity party."

In the time since Nanna slipped me that note, God eventually allowed some of my external circumstances to change. But a deeper, internal adjustment in my heart came first. That seems to be the way He most typically works.

Chapter Nine

God's Plan

*In his heart a man plans his course,
but the LORD determines his steps.*

Proverbs 16:9

Father's Love

by Mildred Hussey,
Xenia, Ohio

"You'll not bring any crazy religion into this house!" My dad yelled at me from his rocking chair in the living room. He jumped up and menacingly shook a clenched fist in my face to emphasize his feelings toward any daughter of his who would take the name of Christ.

Minutes later, I sat in my bedroom listening to my parents shout. I heard the door slam in anger, and then a sudden quiet descended over our home. My eyes welled with tears.

I had always longed for a father who would love me no matter what. Now at the age of fourteen, I finally understood there was just such a Father available to me. He just didn't live at this address.

From the day I was born in that warm little bedroom off the kitchen of our home in Brantford, Ontario, I had seemed a misfit. As if it were not enough that I was not a son, the difficulty of my birth resulted in seemingly mental and physical defects that would cause my father to reject me throughout my childhood. It is not so difficult to survive poverty and want when you have love from both parents. But to understand that your father has no use for you makes it all but impossible to flourish.

One afternoon two years earlier, two smiling people arrived at our front door. They offered a free bus ride to church the next Sunday. Since my father, who did not live with us on a regular basis, was off to parts unknown then, Mother gladly accepted the invitation. I could hardly wait!

The attraction for me was not the church but the bus. It was 1932, and buses were just beginning to become widely used throughout London, where we lived at that time. We were overjoyed to be treated in such grand fashion. I was twelve years old and just beginning to understand my limitations and feelings of inadequacy because I wasn't "right in the head," as my father so often reminded me.

I was immediately in awe at the sight of the huge Victorian mansion that had been renovated and transformed into what would become the center of my life for many years to come. Central Baptist Church and the people in it loved and accepted me just as I was. They didn't seem to notice that I was "crazy in the head" at all. The nervous condition that had hospitalized me twice during my early childhood faded like a bad memory as these people began to love me to Jesus.

It took two years to heal the wounds, but my heart began to break as I understood the love of Christ and my hope of a future in heaven. One Sunday, as tears fell like rain, I slowly walked from the balcony seat of my church home and bowed my knees to Jesus. I knew at that moment there would be no turning back. With this one decision, I knew that a brighter future lay before me. What I had not counted on was my father's anger.

With the door-slamming in our home that day came the end to a bitter chapter of my life. Christ began to write His story on the pages of my heart. My father decided to walk out of our lives, and I began to understand that despite what he said, I had been perfectly created by a God who loved me and had a wonderful purpose for my life. I was not a "nobody" who was crazy in the head. I had more to offer than a nervous stammering tongue and a young life of misery. My heavenly Father began to build the confidence and assurance I would need in order to walk with Him.

God was faithful. The dear people of my church lovingly stood by me and encouraged me through these early teen years when I quit school and got a job to help support our family. They gave me the support I needed to stand strong for Him and not waver or lose hope. When God provided a wonderful young man from that church to be my husband, no one was more surprised than I was. When He called us into the ministry following World War II, I still could not believe it. I often look back on what might have been were it not for the grace of God. I marvel at the person He planned for me to be all along.

Last summer, while staying with my sister in London, I visited the church of my youth. As the sanctuary sat still and empty of people, I found my seat in the balcony and in the very pew where Christ had spoken to me so many years ago. I rested before reliving the moment in time that changed my life forever. Slowly, I rose to my feet. With tears, I made the same pilgrimage to the front of the church. Kneeling in precisely the right place, I gave thanks to God for taking this little nobody, giving her a Father who sent His Son to die for her, and transforming her into a servant for Him.

A life full of opportunity and joy passed before my eyes as I remembered my wedding vows spoken at that very spot with the man of my dreams. I recalled the joy of my husband's ordination to the ministry in that same place and the thrill of walking through those doors as a young mother carrying the first two of my four children to proudly enroll them in the nursery.

And finally I thought of the wonderful ways God has chosen to use my life over these past seventy years of walking with Him. When I left Central Baptist Church that day, it was with renewed gratitude that God gives hope. He holds Himself out to those of us who are hurting from all sorts of hopeless situations, and He calls us to Himself, where we find refuge and strength.

Lessons from the floor

by Lisa Copen,
Poway, California

I went to bed about 2 A.M. and arose at 7:30, literally
creeping to the shower. I was stiff and sore. I had lived
for years with rheumatoid arthritis, and after nearly nine
months without rain in San Diego, it was pouring that
morning. My joints were not pleased with the prospect
of awakening.

My husband was still asleep but would be getting
up soon. He was taking the day off work to accompany
me to a church where I would speak to several chronically ill people about perseverance, faith, taking one
day at a time, and relying on God in the midst of life's
confusions. I was looking forward to it, as I always gain
strength by being around people with illness who
depend fully on God. I felt unprepared, however, as circumstances had given me little opportunity to focus on
or prepare for the presentation. As I showered, I prayed
that God would use me despite my weaknesses. I was
far from perfect, but I was doing the best I could. I
stepped out of the shower and felt my foot begin to
slide. In a flash, I realized that I was going down.

In the nine years that I've lived with arthritis, I can
count the number of times I have sat on the floor. Once,
I was so angry about this illness that was preventing me
from doing something that I rebelled by plopping down

on the floor, knowing that I would be stuck there until my husband came home. Another time I became irritated at the flashing VCR clock that taunted me; while trying to kneel, I lost my balance.

When I was younger and life's circumstances became overwhelming, I got down on my knees to pray. As a teenager when I felt lost and confused, the knees brought reassurance. As a college student, the knees brought comfort that despite the roommate, who wore wanton underwear I didn't even know existed, God was my roommate, too. I expected to wear out lots of kneepads as an adult, but then a chronic illness arrived. The knees now only bring pain and frustration. They remind me of a past life that I can no longer reach despite the floor being just inches away.

I went against instinct to try to catch myself and instead surrendered to the inevitable. I tucked, as the doctor had instructed. "Scratches on the face can heal; broken wrists are not a good thing." I tried to fall toward the carpet but landed on the hard bathroom floor on my left hip and wrist. The stab of pain was great, but even greater was the instant fear that overcame me during the descent. I feared that I would not be able to fulfill my obligations that evening. I could just hear the church announcing, "Our speaker on chronic illness isn't feeling well." That wasn't exactly the kind of credibility that I desired.

After the initial stun of the fall, I slowly gathered my sprawled limbs and curled them close. I sat. I cried. "Why today, Lord?" I asked. "Why *today?*" I demanded! My wrist was not broken, but it was useless for a few days. Did God not realize that I already felt less than confident? Satan had already been tantalizing me, making me feel doubtful about my presentation. *Who do you think you are, giving those people advice? You don't know anything more than they do! You still get discouraged, and you still wonder why you have to deal with all of this.* I didn't need physical bruises and a broken spirit this morning.

Finally, I prayed through my tears. The words were the same. "Why, Lord, why?" But they were filled with a desperate desire to understand, not a demand to an explanation. Then I realized God was determined to remind me that He could always get me on my knees. "Humble yourselves, therefore, under God's mighty hand, that he may lift you up in due time" (1 Peter 5:6).

I was not being humble. My mother would say that God knew I was getting too big for my britches. Despite fears that my message would be less than perfect, I was certain that it wouldn't be difficult. I was a practiced speaker and felt confident in my abilities. I had prayed that God would use my weakness, but was I going to give Him the full credit? My professional self would likely be tempted to credit it to a recent seminar I had attended. Did I want to do well for myself or to really give those people hope? Sure, I am very vocal about giving God the glory, but inside I still feel more pride than I believe would please the Lord.

I had an attitude. I had, I thought, a good excuse for not getting down on my knees. God showed me just how fragile I am without Him. That morning I was too distracted to get the message via a Scripture or a praise song. God needed a stronger delivery method to get my attention. I gradually scooted toward a nearby chair. Was it possible to get up? When I was halfway there, my husband heard me yell and came running.

I hadn't lifted myself up. God had lifted me up, physically and spiritually. It hurt, but I got the message. I understood. I made it to the church, and when they looked at me with their tear-filled eyes, broken spirits, and scarred hearts, I told them I am on the same journey as they are. It may look like I have it all together, but the mascara, pantyhose, and book table do not represent where I was a few hours ago.

Understanding smiles appeared. Skeptical eyes softened with relief that their struggles were normal. "I sat on the floor and cried huge tears just hours ago because of my illness and how it keeps getting in the way of things," I shared with them. "I felt frustrated and mad and annoyed. I felt like a child who can't even get out of the shower properly. I was disheartened because on the one day I needed strength, comfort, and confidence, they were taken from me in an instant. You will fall. We will all have days that we fall in one way or another. But God will pull us all back up. And He knows precisely the unique way to help you up in your circumstances."

Many approached me afterward and said this story made the difference in how their hearts were touched that evening. I am weak, but He is strong.

God has a plan for our lives, and when we head down the wrong path or get in God's way, He's not timid about pulling the floor out from under us. Just when we think we have a good excuse to not get down on our knees, He reminds us we can always get down on our knees because, without humbling ourselves, there is no need for Him to be there to lift us up.

The Eyes Have Spoken

as told to LaRose Karr
by Dixcie Slade,
Sterling, Colorado

I meet a lot of interesting people during my late shift at a convenience store in northeastern Colorado. The day of the attack on the World Trade Center everyone who passed through the Outpost was in total shock.

Planes made emergency landings at the nearest airports. People were told to get off and exit the airport without their baggage. Many were stranded with only the clothes and the money that they had on them. Others rented vehicles and held up signs to see if anyone else might be going their way.

This went on through the night. Late in my shift, two vanloads of people pulled in and everyone piled out. My first impression was that these travelers were quiet, reserved. They wandered up and down the aisles, to the bathroom, then to phones to call family members.

In the background, a man was having trouble staying in control of his emotions. He must have realized I had been watching, and as we made eye contact, I could see there was something in his eyes. He came up to the counter, bent over, and looked me in the eye. His eyes were tired, bloodshot, and misty. He reached for my hand and quietly told me that he and his wife were on their way to see their new great-grandson.

"We were supposed to be on the plane that hit the second tower," he said softly.

The hair on my neck and arms stood up. I searched his eyes for any type of joke. He said that as he and his wife prepared to board that plane, he smelled something dead and had a feeling of utter coldness. He told his wife that he could not stay on the plane, so they departed. Several other people who overheard him decided to leave, too.

"When we got off, there were seven people behind us," his wife added. She had looked down the aisle of the plane. "Several others were grabbing their carry-on luggage and following us. More people outside the gate decided not to get on either. I counted a total of fourteen people. Fourteen of us felt in our very souls that we should not be on that plane."

For a moment, it seemed the world stopped. No one spoke. The building grew quiet.

Then a customer walked up to the couple and broke the silence. "It was an act of God that made you get off." Then he placed his hand on the man's shoulder and invited him and his wife to dinner.

I don't know their names or where they were going, but that man, his wife, and a dozen or more others had been spared by God for reasons yet unknown. The man and his wife were heading to see a new life. Perhaps that was reason enough.

The Provision

by Sheryl Pellatiro,
Troy, Michigan

When I graduated from high school, I had no plans for my future. I hadn't thought about it, except that college was out of the question. I didn't think I would be accepted because my grade point average was extremely low. Plus I hated high school. So why would I want to torture myself through college?

God had other plans.

By the time I was twenty-one, I had a full-time job, a new car, and the comfort and security of living at home with my parents. And God was beginning to work in my heart. I had such a deep thirst and hunger for His Word that every day I would go home from work, barricade myself in my bedroom, and read and soak up biblical truths. I didn't have a care in the world; all I could think about was God. So I should not have been surprised that He had a greater plan for my life.

While sitting at my desk, minding my own business one workday, God whispered in my ear to go to the local Bible college and pick up an application. All the way home, I kept telling Him that if this was His will for my life, then He had a lot of obstacles to overcome.

"Lord, how could I ever be accepted?" I asked. "How could I ever afford to go? What about my parents? I pay room and board, and they certainly can't afford to send me, so what will they say about this?"

As these questions rolled off my lips, my heart churned with excitement and anticipation. As always, God overcame every obstacle. I began Bible college. I could see God working in my life. For the first time, I did well academically.

By the second year of college, my funds were running dry. In fact, one Sunday during Christmas break, I sat on my bed crying. I had absolutely no money to return for the winter semester, and registration was four days away.

"Sheryl, maybe you should take a semester off. Work, and return to school when you save some money," my mom proposed.

"No," I insisted. "God wouldn't send me to Bible college and then not provide."

That night after church, I went out with some Christian friends. As we sat around the table talking, I asked them to pray for me. I shared my story. One of the men asked me how much I needed.

"Four hundred dollars," I sighed.

"Sheryl, you're not going to believe this, but I have a fund set aside for God's work," he explained. "I want to give it to you so that you can continue your education. Right now, I have exactly four hundred dollars in the bank. It's yours."

We all sat in total awe of God.

I graduated at age twenty-six, and God was my provider every step of the way. My faith was strengthened as I continued to see God work out all the details. It reminds me of the verse that says, "The one who calls you is faithful and he will do it" (1 Thessalonians 5:24).

Friendship Bread

by Amy Jenkins,
Wauwatosa, Wisconsin

My mom dropped off a baggie with taupe-colored goop in it and a recipe for "Friendship Bread." It takes ten days to make this cakelike bread, which is reported to have Amish origins.

Every twelve hours, I was to shake the bag, and on some days add something to it. It was imperative, or so said the instructions, that this be done on schedule. By day four, I was muttering about how stupid this was. "No, I can't sleep late; I have to get up early to shake my friendship bag." Seven P.M.? "No, we can't stop for ice cream."

When we went to the movies, I took my tote bag containing the required ingredients. While Harrison Ford fought a battle on *Air Force One,* I met my responsibility. At the appropriate time, I poured in a cup of sugar and shook the mixture. As I peeked over my shoulder to be sure that the usher wouldn't catch me, I wondered what they would do if they did catch me. I imagined being banned from the Capital Theater. Perhaps they'd post a drawing of a mixing bowl and spoon with a red circle and a line through it. Harrison and I accomplished our missions successfully.

On the last day, I poured my creation into a mixing bowl with the other ingredients to make four loaves. That's where I made my critical mistake. I missed the part where I was first supposed to divide the liquid into five bags and just use one bag at a time. Since I had already poured the whole bag of liquid in, I was committed to baking all twenty loaves of bread. *What in heaven's name will I do with twenty loaves of bread?* I lamented silently.

In the middle of baking the last batch, I heard the radio announcer report that Habitat for Humanity was starting their housing blitz the next day and was asking for volunteers. I was pleased to learn I could volunteer to sponsor a snack.

The bread was moist, sweet, and topped with a crunchy cinnamon mixture. I sliced up nineteen loaves, spread them attractively on trays, wrapped them in plastic wrap, and took them to the Habitat work site.

Every year since, they have asked me to sponsor a snack. In recent years, I've brought muffins, fruit, and cupcakes. They still ask me to bring that delicious friendship bread, but I don't have a bag of squishy goop. I have no idea how it starts—someone would have to give me a batch, exactly eleven days before the start of the blitz. What's the chance of that happening—again?

Last July my new neighbor came over as I was baking muffins. She asked me what I was doing. When I explained about the building blitz, she asked me how I got involved in Habitat for Humanity. After the story of my accidental volunteer work, she told me, "The only way that story could be true is if God had planned it.

"And God must have planted me here as your new neighbor as well," she said, shaking her head in further amazement as she went on to tell me that she and her mother's friends pass around the friendship batter every year, and that I should look for a baggie of fermenting goop about the beginning of next July, just in time for the next Habitat building blitz.

Angel in a Snowsuit

by Ellen Javernick,
Loveland, Colorado

Time didn't have much meaning for Mrs. Ramsey. Her only daughter, a darling little girl with long black braids and a sparkling smile, died of leukemia when she was in second grade, and her husband died just a few years later. She felt old, unloved, and unneeded. One day was pretty much the same as the next, and Valentine's Day crept up almost unnoticed.

She was surprised one February morning when she answered the door and saw a rosy-cheeked boy of five or six standing on her doorstep. He was stuffed into a bright blue snowsuit. In his mittened hands he held a bunch of cheery red carnations, "and baby's breath, too," marveled Mrs. Ramsey. The little boy pushed the bouquet at Mrs. Ramsey and dashed off down the street before Mrs. Ramsey had time to protest that she had no one to send her flowers. She carried the bouquet inside and looked for a card that might explain the gift. She found a red construction-paper heart in the folds of the paper wrapped around the flowers. "We Love You" was carefully printed on the handmade card. It was signed "the children of Edgemont school."

Mrs. Ramsey didn't know quite what to make of the gift. *I haven't,* she admitted to herself, *been especially nice to the Edgemont boys and girls.* She'd even gotten crabby and scolded the children who walked past her house on their way to school. She'd called the principal to complain about their noisy laughter on the playground and shaken her broom at them when they stomped through puddles on her sidewalk. She was furious when she found a small snow angel on the front lawn. Why would they send her a Valentine card?

She promised herself she'd try to be more pleasant. She began chatting with the children when they walked past. She learned their names and admired the work they carried home. In the spring she started a garden. "So the children would have something pretty to look at," she explained. The following fall she walked over to school and asked the secretary if the school could use a volunteer to help with reading.

Mrs. Ramsey was already a permanent fixture at Edgemont School when I came as a new first-grade teacher. A gaunt but gracious woman, she seemed to spend almost as much time at school as I did. Her smile so warmed the little people she tutored that they begged, "Please, please, can Mrs. Ramsey work with me?" She patted kids' heads and praised their paintings. She called the kindergartners her little angels. She was such a popular volunteer and so effective that I assumed she must be a retired teacher. One day I asked my older teaching partner how long Mrs. Ramsey had been helping at Edgemont.

Allison told me the amazing story of the Valentine card. "Which teacher thought to send her the Valentine flowers?" I asked. Allison laughed. "That's about the strangest part of the story. Miss Perlee was teaching kindergarten then, and she decided it would be nice to send Valentine thank-yous to some of the neighborhood volunteers. She got one of the grocery stores to give her a good price on carnations and then had the children divide them into bouquets. The kids cut out the hearts and copied the words. She gave the flowers to children to drop off on their way home. Little Davey Hamilton was supposed to deliver the flowers to a volunteer on Mrs. Ramsey's street but had trouble with his numbers. Instead of leaving the flowers for the faithful volunteer who lived at 741, he took them to Mrs. Ramsey at 714!"

"Did she ever find out? Mrs. Ramsey, I mean," I asked Allison.

"Davey admitted his mistake," said Allison, "when he was in sixth grade."

Mrs. Ramsey said it wasn't a mistake. "God knew exactly what He was doing the day He sent me an angel in a snowsuit."

Honey, Will You Come Here?

by Leone A. Browning,
Fairfield, Washington

Previously published in The Standard, *September 23, 1984,* Evangel, *September 13, 1987,* The Helping Hand, *July-August 1995, and* Live, *January 16, 2000.*

Always remember that God not only allows U-turns for yourself but also provides opportunities for you to help others make U-turns. I remember a time when my husband was hospitalized and God gave me just such an opportunity.

As I entered my husband's hospital room, I heard the soft moaning of his elderly roommate. After several moments of waiting, he pressed his button on the call light. It was a long time before an angry nurse stomped into the room, turned out the light, and scolded the little old man for bothering her. She left without asking what he wanted.

Before long, he was calling the nurses again for pain pills, then for a drink of water, a change of position, or anything else that would relieve his discomfort. After listening to several encounters with the nurses, I tried to relieve his restlessness and make him comfortable in any way I possibly could to try and keep him from calling for help so often.

He was grateful and quiet the times I massaged his neck gently, fluffed his pillow, or dialed a phone number for him. Sometimes I just listened to him talk. I was concerned for his soul as he revealed some things about his lifestyle. I prayed for him many times.

His intense blue eyes and gratitude reminded me of the days I spent with my own father before he passed away. He even called me "honey" in the same appreciative voice that Papa had.

One morning I heard him ask for a chaplain. The chaplain listened as the man said, "I don't have long to live. I need spiritual help." The chaplain had prayer with him, but the little man still seemed unhappy.

By this time, my husband's roommate started asking me for small favors. The next day he said, "Honey, will you come here?"

I went to his side expecting to help in some small way. I was surprised when he asked, "Do you know how to pray?"

"Yes, I talk to God often," I stammered. "What do you need?"

He answered weakly, "I don't think I have much time left in this old world, and I'm not sure I'm ready to die. Would you please pray for me? I need to know that God has forgiven me for all my sins."

I simply asked God to give him inner peace and the assurance that his sins were forgiven. Then I suggested that he ask Jesus Christ to forgive him and come into his heart. He moved his lips as he prayed silently. Then he looked up and smiled and wiped a tear from his cheek.

Somehow, I didn't feel pressed to say anything else. I knew God would deal with him better than I could. I slipped away quietly, praying that his need would be met. I noticed that he was not as restless and needed less attention the rest of the day.

The next morning he once more called, "Honey, will you come here?" Sometimes I got tired and almost wished he would quit calling and let me read or crochet, but I felt an urgency about his requests and went to his side. He reached out for my hand and smiled, even though his eyes were filled with tears.

"Do you know what happened to me yesterday?" he asked.

"No, I have no idea. Would you care to tell me?"

"I gave my life to the Lord while you prayed for me. I'm the happiest I've been for years." He beamed.

I patted his bony hand and thanked him for sharing his joy with me.

"Would you continue to pray for me? I have so many broken pieces to put back together," he confided.

I assured him that God would mend his shattered life and that I would pray for him.

Our conversation was interrupted when two ministers entered the room to visit my husband. Before they left, they stopped to ask the little old man how things were with him.

"Just fine," he responded happily. "I settled everything with God yesterday when the lady over there prayed with me. I'm ready to meet my Maker now."

How my heart rejoiced at hearing him speak those words. Once more I whispered, "Thank You, Lord, for giving me this opportunity. Help me never to fail You," and suddenly I understood why the Lord had placed me here. . .for such a time as this.

Chapter
Ten

Forever Friends

"A new command I give you: Love one another.
As I have loved you, so you must love one another. . . .
All men will know that you are my disciples,
if you love one another."

John 13:34–35

Mae

by Margaret Hoffman,
Williamsport, Pennsylvania

One of the dear saints of God who stands out in my mind and personal life was Mae, the mother-in-law of a good friend. She was a farmer's wife who raised eleven children. Her experiences gave her a boldness that I often found comical.

She loved the Lord dearly, and even the pastor of the church at that time would come to her for wisdom. She was as wide as she was tall and never took any guff from her multitude of grandchildren, and she loved them in the way that only Mae could.

When I was a young mother in my twenties with two little toddlers in hand, I would make my way across several farmers' fields, through the rolling hills of Pennsylvania, to attend a Bible study that Mae had in her home every Tuesday morning. The grass and fields were always covered with dew. The children and I would carry a change of socks or slippers to wear while our shoes and socks dried out by her fireplace.

In the summer months, all her grandchildren congregated at her home. It was not uncommon for friends and strangers to find themselves snapping beans on her porch while she testified of God's goodness to all who were listening.

After the death of her husband, Mae's health began

to fail. At that time my oldest daughter, then sixteen, was an aide at the nursing home where Mae was sent. Diabetes claimed her eyesight and one leg, and Alzheimer's claimed her mind. She was thin and helpless.

Each day my daughter would come home and tell me of Mae's digression. I was such a coward, not wanting to see this previously strong woman in such a condition. It broke my heart to even think of it. Finally I gave in and went to visit her. It quickly became a habit to visit her two to three times a week.

Mae never recognized me. On better days I could be her mother, sister, or child. On bad days she would just lie in her bed with little movement. She was so tiny and weak, nothing like the woman who once chased that feisty rooster across the barnyard with a broom. Yet when I would open my Bible and read Scripture to her, her mind was right there, and she recited along with me with a smile on her face. Her reality began and ended with God.

She used to tell me how important it was to read and memorize God's Word because there might come a day when we would not be able to do that. We would have to rely on what was burned into our hearts. She was right. At this time in her life, she was a living testimony of that very thing.

One of the last times I saw Mae before she went home to glory, I had had a particularly hectic week—a week that only a single parent can know. I was exhausted, discouraged, and feeling pretty beat-up by the world. Being with Mae was a haven. I sat in the chair beside her and opened my Bible on her bed, as usual.

Before I knew it, I had leaned forward, resting my face on my Bible, and was soon fast asleep. I woke later to the nudge of a gentle nurse's aide, my daughter. I was drooling all over God's Word. Mae was stroking my hair and singing softly, "I've Got a Home in Glory Land." Though her mind was gone, her spirit comforted me. She reached out through the veil of frailty to serve someone else.

My humble attempts at ministering to this dear woman failed miserably in comparison to how she had ministered to me. Even in her frailty, she was able to shine for God. Even though her mind and body were so fragile at the end of her life, her spirit soared. I was never able to convey to her what her testimony did for me and my family at that time, but I know it added a jewel to her crown in glory.

A Woman's Journey

Mercy's Time

by Julie Saffrin,
Excelsior, Minnesota

She was nearly my mother-in-law. That she is not had nothing to do with her. The two years we knew each other, Doris was easy to know. I was nineteen. She, in her late fifties.

She welcomed my presence into her son's life, treated me like a daughter in hers. Our mutual love for her son was our commonality and made our bond strong.

Invited to their world, I shared meals and trips to the cabin. A year later, a depleted box of tissue accompanied Doris and me on the way home after we left her son at boot camp.

To fend off long winter nights, I visited her after work. We had warm talks of possibilities. She, a patient right-hander, taught me, a left-hander with dreams of marriage, to crochet a bedspread. I even helped her pick out a puppy at the humane society; Doris named her Precious.

When the engagement was announced, her gifts of a silverware chest and milk-glass butter dish started the hope chest. Though she often said she was a terrible cook, my first recipe of Mexican stew, which I still make, came from her.

When the engagement was broken, so, too, was my friendship with Doris. Awkward and young, I didn't

A Woman's Journey

know how to say good-bye. So I didn't.

On occasion, in the twenty years since, she would come to mind. As hard as I tried, I could not put her out of my head. I knew I would never forgive myself if something happened to her before I said I was sorry for my rude behavior.

On a Florida vacation, while I read a novel filled with estrangements and reconciliations, she visited my thoughts again. Whether Doris chose to forgive me or not, the inevitable was here. It was time to apologize for the abrupt severing of our friendship.

I had no idea where she lived but knew her sister, Elsie, lived in town. A long walk with my index finger through the phone directory found her. It took me two weeks to muster the courage to call.

Elsie informed me that the years had been harsh to Doris. She had gone through a divorce, several seizures, brain surgery, and was now in the final stage of emphysema. When I asked if it would be all right to write her, her sister said that it would be fine.

Now that I had permission I was terrified. I had broken her son's heart and burst a seemingly perfect dream of togetherness. Surely she must hate me. *Certainly no good will come from a simple handwritten apology,* I thought.

A sleepless week went by. It was no use. Until I put pen to paper, there would be no peace in my heart.

Lord, give me the words to convey my sorriness, was my quiet plea. "Dear Doris, I know it's been many years since you and I last had contact," I began. It took until page three to get to my reason for writing. "I know when I broke his heart, I broke part of yours. Knowing you like I once did, you probably forgave me years ago, but what good is an apology that no one hears? I'm sorry for the pain and the way I ended it all," I wrote. I asked for forgiveness; if she found it in her heart to do so, I wanted to hear it.

A week went by, two, before her familiar curly handwriting appeared in my mailbox. The envelope was heavy. My fears resurfaced. I prepared for a severe lecture.

"You can't know what your letter has done for me," she wrote. "Came at the right time, too." Her letter was delightful. She gladly accepted my apology, forgave me, recalled some happy times, even asked for a recipe. Her words lightened a burden I had carried too long.

As I put the letter back in the envelope, a picture of Precious slipped out. On the back she had written, "Remember when you went with me to pick her out? She died last year. I miss her so." I thought of that dog. Like the Mexican stew, it made me happy that a part of our togetherness had carried into Doris's life, too.

God's merciful timing played a part in Doris and me settling things. Two months later, her sister called to tell me the sad news that Doris had passed away. I'm grateful God knew I needed to say good-bye.

Chapter Eleven

Forgiveness

*"And when you stand praying, if you hold anything
against anyone, forgive him, so that your Father
in heaven may forgive you your sins."*

Mark 11:25

A Lesson in Forgiveness

by Joan Clayton,
Portales, New Mexico

Appeared in Teachers in Focus, *March 1999, and* Seasons
of a Woman's Heart: A Daybook of Stories and Inspiration, *Starburst Publishing.*

Annie's day started out all wrong. The other children complained as they kept reporting instances of the insults and mistreatment she was inflicting. I took Annie aside and whispered quietly. She vehemently denied any wrongdoing. When Eddie reported that Annie had pinched him (the redness of his arm testified to the fact), I asked Annie to stay in the room with me during noon recess.

Annie came in at noon, sat down, and finished her math. Eddie came in to finish his math, too. They both brought their papers to me about the same time. I checked them and said to her, "Do you have something to say to Eddie?"

She looked at Eddie. "I'm so sorry. I don't know why I did that. I wish. . .I really wish I wouldn't do things like that."

"That's okay." Eddie's chin was quivering, but it was over. . .complete forgiveness, never to be remembered again.

The other children came in from lunch recess and we all settled down for story time. I noticed Annie didn't join us. Since she had offended so many other children, she was holding back, but deep down, I felt she wanted to be part of the group.

I pulled her close and said, "Do you have something you want to say to the other children?" I breathed a sigh of relief as she walked to the front of the class. But when she stood in front of the group, she remained silent and became hostile again. I asked Annie to please return to her seat and told her that when she had something to say, she could rejoin the group, praying all the while I was doing the right thing.

As I read the last page of the story to the children, Annie came to me and whispered, "I have something to say." She began, "I'm sorry I've been mean to all of you. I'm sorry I pulled your hair. I didn't mean to kick you. I'm sorry I spit on you. I really don't want to be that way!"

Spontaneously, the children cheered and clapped. Annie smiled as she sat down and nestled in among the group. Even though the children had not mistreated her, they began to say, "We're sorry, too! We didn't treat you right either." It happened just that simply, over and done with. Case closed. Yes, other infractions of the rules might occur, but they must be dealt with as they happened. This particular incident ended.

When do we lose that ability to forgive? Where in that transition from childhood to adulthood do we hang on to not forgiving? We visualize instant replays of some incident that happened months, even years ago. Every time it is replayed, the unjust wounds, the anger that festers in the unhealed places in our minds, is felt again and again.

I made a U-turn that day. I resolved to choose to have the forgiving, loving spirit of a child. I learned to look within myself. Even though I thought the other children had not offended Annie, they too searched within themselves, seeking to make things right.

I'm so thankful for children. They continue to teach me, just as Scripture does when it refers to their innocent wisdom: "Of such is the kingdom of heaven" (Matthew 19:14 NKJV).

Please Forgive Me

by Amy Givler,
Monroe, Louisiana

Originally published in Moody Magazine, *September/ October 2000.*

Early one Saturday morning, my friend Susan called. "Amy, if you're not too busy," she said, her normally controlled voice quavering, "I'd like to get together with you sometime today."

Her voice told me she was fighting to control her emotions. I assumed she needed advice. I wasn't surprised she would turn to me since I'm the leader of a small weekly Bible study she attends. Still, she tends to keep her emotions tightly capped, and she doesn't often ask for help. Our friendship had developed slowly.

"Of course we can get together," I said. "You name the time."

"I'll be there in an hour," she said.

I felt a surge of compassion for her as I hung up, and I wondered what she needed to share. The week before, another member of the group sought me out to discuss how she should respond to her overbearing mother. I felt the glimmer of a prompting to pray for Susan before she arrived, but I banished that thought. Surely I could handle giving a little advice on my own. Hadn't I taken a couple of counseling classes? Instead, I spent the hour relishing the thought that the Bible study and my leadership seemed to be meeting a need in these women's lives.

When Susan arrived, we decided to find a place to talk at the park across the street. We walked silently. She kept her head down and her lips compressed as I indulged her need for quiet. Once we were across from each other at a picnic table, I calmly waited for her to speak.

"I want you to know that the Bible study you lead means a lot to me," she began, "and I guess if I didn't care about it I wouldn't be here right now. I would just make excuses week after week and not show up."

I swallowed hard, and my throat suddenly felt dry. Not trusting my voice, I nodded for her to continue. This didn't sound like a prelude to asking for advice.

"But when I left the Bible study last Thursday, Amy, I never wanted to set foot in your house again."

What was she saying? My chest felt tight as I drew a sharp breath. Was she angry at me? I searched her eyes for clues, but they were focused on the tabletop.

"Before Thursday's lesson formally began," she said softly, "we were talking about year-round school. You lashed out at me when I said I saw some advantages to it."

My eyes widened, and I felt a flare of annoyance. *Year-round school? How could she possibly see the slightest advantage to it? It tears families apart. Of course I'm going to speak out against it.*

"But when I taught school I saw how children forgot so much over the summer," she continued. "Year-round school keeps education fresh."

My mind raced as she methodically explained her position. How had I responded to her on Thursday? She must be overreacting. Surely I had been gracious. . .or had I? With a painful pang my memory cleared: I had cut her off midsentence and ridiculed her opinion. But I believed my position was right. Doesn't that count? I felt a fragile flicker of guilt as she continued speaking. I tried to quench it, but it grew larger. Slowly, slowly, I admitted to myself that I had been wrong to be harsh and inflexible. My dominating the time before our study hadn't exactly allowed for a smooth transition to biblical truths. I tuned back in to Susan.

"I may not be teaching school right now," she was saying, "but I have a degree in education and I think about current issues."

I struggled to grasp the scope of my offense. I had been obnoxious. I told myself that I'd probably have to apologize sometime, maybe after I'd thought about it for a few days. But then I would explain to her why I had said what I'd said. Maybe I could still convince her of my point of view.

Susan was relating how crushed she felt. As she continued to speak, I suddenly realized I had been nasty to Susan and I needed to apologize today. Right now. And I shouldn't say a single word in my own defense. I grappled with that conviction. Couldn't I just present my perspective?

Then, hesitantly, I recognized my behavior as sinful. As I did, a proverb came to mind: "He who conceals his sins does not prosper, but whoever confesses and renounces them finds mercy" (Proverbs 28:13).

Clearly, I needed to ask her forgiveness and not make excuses for my behavior. Susan had stopped speaking and was looking down at her folded hands on the table. I drew a deep breath before taking the plunge.

"Susan," I said, "I was wrong on Thursday, and I ask you to forgive me. I attacked you when you offered your opinion, and I'm sorry for that. Will you forgive me for acting like such a jerk?"

Susan looked up with a hint of a smile. "Yes, I forgive you, Amy."

I stretched out my hand on the table, and when she grasped it I squeezed hers. Her eyes glistened, and I blinked back tears. The walk back was just as silent as our walk to the park had been, but this time I was absorbed in prayer. *God, will You forgive me? I hurt You, too, by treating the women You entrusted to my care so shabbily.*

Later that day, as I considered how much courage it took for Susan to confront me, I wondered whether other members of the group had been wounded by my overbearing remarks. I called each one to ask her forgiveness. And as I feared, each one knew what I was talking about. Each one forgave me.

Before our next meeting, I began a new approach to leadership. During the week, instead of brief prayers for the women and our time together, I committed each woman and her needs to God. I decided to stop trusting in my natural abilities to help these women and begin relying solely on God. And so, as the women grow closer to God, He alone receives the glory, which is exactly as it should be.

Night of Terror

as told to
Angela Keith Benedict,
Van Nuys, California

It was late and the Laundromat was deserted, but I wasn't afraid. My apartment was just across the alley, and I could run in and do my wash and be back home in a matter of minutes. I had done it a hundred times before.

I didn't hear the two men until they were directly behind me; then it was too late. I started to scream but was hit in the face by one of my assailants as the other one grabbed me.

"One more sound and you're dead," he hissed.

I was literally dragged to a car waiting in the alley and thrown into the backseat. I was too terrified to do anything, and there was nowhere to go. I was raped by both of them, but they had hit me so many times by then that I was literally numb and hardly aware of what was going on. It was like a horrible nightmare, and yet I knew I was awake and it was truly happening.

Eventually we drove off. One man sat with me in the backseat while the other drove. They were planning to kill me; that much was apparent from the snatches of conversation I could understand in my state of shock.

God, help me, I prayed. Praying made all the difference. *I'm in Your hands now,* I told Him. Despite the physical pain and mental anguish, I felt a sense of peace when I turned the situation over to Him.

We were speeding through the night, evidently searching for just the right canyon or ravine in which to dump me, when I heard the most beautiful sound I have ever heard. Piercing the night air was a patrol car's siren. I could see the flashing red lights in the rearview mirror.

"Play it straight," the man sitting next to me advised the driver as he pulled over. "I'll take care of the cop."

We had been stopped for speeding, and as I sat there the policeman asked to see a driver's license, plus the registration. There was a gun in my ribs, and I knew for certain that this man was not kidding and would shoot.

Suddenly, the gun was pulled away from me and aimed straight at the policeman's head.

"Look out!" I screamed.

The gun went off, and a bullet went into my neck and out the other side.

From police records and the newspaper story, I learned that the man in the backseat was arrested on the spot, and the other man somehow managed to drive off, only to be captured later.

I was taken to a hospital where emergency surgery was performed to save my life. If it had not been for the surgeon's skill, I would have passed into eternity that night.

Months later, the case came to trial. Physically my body had completely healed, but emotionally I had more than a few scars. The trial didn't help a great deal. Despite my testimony of what had happened, plus the account given by the policeman—even despite the previous records of my attackers—it was difficult getting a conviction.

The defense attorney actually tried to make it look

as if I had somehow enticed those men in the Laundromat and was at least partially to blame for what happened to me. Fortunately, the jury didn't buy it, and both men were given lengthy jail terms.

That isn't the end of the story. I had meant it when I told God I was putting my life in His hands the night of my attack. I became active in a Bible-preaching church, was baptized, and for the first time in my life actively sought God's will for my life through faith in Christ.

But something kept bothering me. Verses like, "Bless those who persecute you" (Romans 12:14) began to haunt me. I couldn't forget the two men who had assaulted me, and every time I thought of them my thoughts were not kind thoughts. They were full of hate and bitterness.

"Don't I have a right to hate them?" I asked myself. "They would have killed me if it hadn't been for the police."

Forgive them, a voice kept saying to me. *Pray for them. They need the Lord!*

"But I can't!" I answered.

You can do all things through Me, came the reply.

It was difficult, but I began to pray for those men. At first the prayers were noncommittal, just, "God, I pray for Lennie and Jack." I knew I needed to do more, however. Prayer should be specific, my pastor has always said. "God, I pray for the salvation of Lennie and Jack." Then I paused. "Help me to forgive them."

Those five words were the beginning of my inner healing, my emotional healing, for as I began to forgive them and pray for their souls, the Lord went to work in my life. My whole outlook changed, and friends tell me I became a more radiant Christian. I could even talk about my experience and share my testimony without becoming upset, something which wasn't possible before.

They were not just empty words either; I had honestly forgiven Lennie and Jack. I continued to pray for their salvation.

In the Los Angeles area, we have many excellent Christian television and radio programs. Some of these include a ministry within the penal institutions. I was listening to such a program one weekend when the name being spoken registered. I couldn't believe I had heard correctly and even called the station to find out.

There was nothing wrong with my hearing. Lennie had indeed received Christ as his Savior while in prison!

Difficult to accept Lennie, the man who had raped me and then shot me, as my brother in Christ? I thought it would be, but it wasn't. In fact, I firmly believe that it was through the power of prayer that Lennie gave his heart to the Lord.

I stay out of Laundromats late at night, yes, but I can truthfully say that God used this terrifying U-turn experience to bring me closer to Him. His ways are not our ways, and we may not always understand the directions our lives take. Yet when we place ourselves in the hands of God we can rest assured that our heavenly Navigator knows exactly what He is doing.

God truly is "in control."

The Long Miracle

by Debbye Butler,
Indianapolis, Indiana

I knew the story of Jesus as well as any little girl could know it. I knew my prayers—even the Lord's Prayer. My big sister taught me that. And I knew the words to "Jesus Loves Me." But I was still lost. . .to a world of seclusion, distrust, and shame at my tender age. *Jesus, do You love me?* I wondered. *Am I bad?*

When I was a tiny six-year-old girl, I became the victim of a perversion that took place regularly in my home: sexual molestation by a live-in older stepbrother. He was a teenager when he abused me, but because I was so small for my age and he was older and bigger, I thought of him as an adult. And I bought into his lies and sin. I did whatever he asked. Things I would never consider even with a marriage partner.

One day, I started hiding in my bedroom closet. I stuffed myself there like a piece of lost clothing that gets dropped in a lost-and-found box. The dark closet became my safe haven—a refuge from this unspeakable ugliness that wouldn't go away for six long years. That's a lifetime to a child.

He made my world dark and scary instead of light and playful. He made me hate my childhood. I wanted to be a "good girl" but grew up feeling quite the opposite even after the abuse stopped. I was bad. I was ugly.

I was unlovable. I believed I deserved every horrible thing that happened to me.

And that's the ugly preface to this, the long miracle of my life.

It was in that closet that God filled me with His strength so I could emotionally survive this childhood travesty that haunts thousands of youngsters each year. I can't explain how I knew, even as a little girl, that God would get me through this never-ending nightmare. But there was no question in my mind—not then, and not now. I knew instinctively about God. If I had no other calm in my young life, I had spiritual peace.

It frightens me to think about the choices I may have made without God's abiding love and strength that enveloped me. The only reason I survived the trauma was that He was present. Otherwise, I most surely would have become addicted to drugs or alcohol, been promiscuous, or perhaps even suicidal. I did not have the wherewithal to deliver myself from the bondage of this shame. It came from a higher power.

I always have known that God did not put me through this, but that He got me through it. Romans 5:3–5 could not be more applicable: "We. . .rejoice in our sufferings, because we know that suffering produces perseverance; perseverance, character; and character, hope. And hope does not disappoint us, because God has poured out his love into our hearts by the Holy Spirit, whom he has given us."

I have always thanked Jesus for helping me persevere through the silent suffering. What I failed to do all these decades was truly have a forgiving heart toward the man who shattered my childhood. Deep inside, I've wanted to forgive him for a long time, knowing it's what Jesus wants. He said in Luke 6:37, "Forgive, and you will be forgiven."

So I've spent the past few years praying for Christ to help me say—and mean—those healing words, "I forgive you." Part of my prayer was to ask God not to call me home until I was able to forgive the few people who have hurt me to the core of my being—the serious, life-altering sorts of hurts. I didn't want to go to my grave, much less heaven, with a speck of hate in my heart.

I hadn't communicated with my perpetrator for more than thirty-one years, but we share someone special in our lives—our sister—whose presence in my world has made an incomprehensible contribution to my faith and life. She told me for years that as an adult her brother dedicated his life to the Lord, but my bitterness would not allow me to believe it.

My sister lives out of state. While she was visiting in the summer of 1999, she said she had something to tell me. "He's entered counseling for his past sinful sexual behavior against you," she revealed. "And he has dedicated his life to serving Jesus."

I don't know if he had other victims; I'd always suspected it. Sex offenders usually have a lifetime pattern. And I don't know what made him decide to seek counseling. But knowing he finally admitted what he had done made all the difference. It was all I needed to know—that he had confessed this sin, not to me, but to others—most especially to Jesus, the Great Healer.

The next words out of my mouth came as unexpectedly to me as they did to my sister. Teary-eyed and with a cracked voice, I said, "Tell him I forgive him." I meant it.

She left the room momentarily. I suspect it was to do exactly what I was doing: crying, regaining composure, and telling God, "Thank You for this healing moment." She delivered my message weeks later, to which her brother replied, "Tell her I'm sorry for any pain I caused her."

When I look back on my life, I remember that somehow I miraculously got stuffed in a lost-and-found box. We all have one. It could be anywhere from a street corner to a courtroom, a sailboat to a jail cell, a hospital bed to a church pew on a decision Sunday. For me, it was a bedroom closet. I was quietly united with Christ, who began preparing me to walk in His way and do His work, equipping me with His abundant strength for survival and walking side by side with me on a journey toward forgiveness that would take decades.

Nearly two years after that conversation, my sister and I were together for another life-changing event. Our dad lay dying, and the entire family was summoned to his bedside. It meant I would be face-to-face with my stepbrother for the first time in thirty-three years. He approached me in the nursing home hallway.

"Debbye, can I talk to you a minute?" he asked gently. "I want to tell you I'm sorry for what I did and ask you to forgive me."

"I do," I replied. "It's in the past."

We both were healed, and the burden of sin miraculously lifted from our shoulders. Once more, my Lord wiped my tears, held my hand, and showed me the way. He took my heart of stone and gave me a new one just as He had promised.

Through the power of our Lord and Savior, I am a little girl lost. . .and found.

Chapter Twelve

God's Love

We love because he first loved us.

1 John 4:19

His Little Girl

by Barbara Curtis,
Petalume, California

I remember the day my dad left. He knelt and hugged me and cried. The skimpy dress of a five-year-old girl couldn't protect me from the chill that gathered around my arms and legs. The scratchy, tickly whiskers— would I feel them no more? The arms that felt so safe— would they be gone forever?

What would it be like not to have a father?

The years to come provided harsh answers to those questions. Mine was not a carefree childhood. Shuffled with two brothers between foster homes, relatives, and— when things worked out—my mother, I toughed out the hard times.

My innocence gave way early on to a cynic's world-view: Don't depend on anyone, and no one will disappoint you.

As anyone without a father will agree, the loss doesn't end when you grow up. The scars are like the glossy, too-tight skin that grows over a healing wound. Beneath the protective cover lies too much tenderness.

For the longest time, I didn't know about the tenderness. I tended the gloss—taking control of my future, acquiring a good education, rising above the pattern of my family's past. I guess you might say with no one to believe in, I learned to believe in myself.

Only when this unsustainable strategy dropped me down-and-out—and more alone than ever—did I finally face my fatherlessness.

So it was in my thirties—sensing what was missing was spiritual—that I finally launched a search for God. For someone like me, the New Age movement held enormous appeal. Here I could wander into nooks and crannies, borrowing this and that to construct an image of God that meshed with my own deficiencies. Crippled by the lack of a real father in my life, seeing God only as some remote and impersonal force, my hope was that through understanding, I could appropriate the force—recognizing "God within me"—then manipulate it to find happiness.

With my eyes on the ground, happiness was as high as I could aim my sight. I wouldn't have thought to seek His love.

And yet how amazingly unconditional and enduring His love remained for me. No matter how I misunderstood Him, He continued to understand me. How patiently He waited as I wandered—for seven more years protecting me from harm, continuing to draw me nearer, gradually softening my heart.

My husband helped to soften me—though I never could have told him then. Watching him father our children was like peeking through a frosted pane into a warm and cozy home within.

Although seeing my children experience a happy childhood was the next best thing to having one myself, how I wished sometimes to climb inside and receive that kind of love myself.

Oh, how ready I was the moment I first heard God was my Father! How easy it was to believe He loved me, had a plan for my life, and through Jesus Christ would have a relationship with me. Of course, I wanted a Father!

At last, I was Someone's little girl!

To this day, ten years later, I cannot approach God intellectually, only as a child. Yet He has never asked me to do more. With no reservations, I feel His love: "Though my father and mother forsake me, the LORD will receive me" (Psalm 27:10). Is it not a miracle that someone who missed an earthly father's love can be healed to receive the love of the heavenly Father? But isn't He Jehovah, the God who heals?

The greatest privilege of all is to call Him Abba, Father.

According to *Vine's Word Dictionary,* " 'Abba' is a word framed by the lips of infants and betokens unreasoning trust. Father expresses an intelligent apprehension of the relationship. The two together express the love and intelligent confidence of a child."

I remember once before he left, my father carrying me home in his arms as blood gushed from a jagged cut on my foot. I was four and frightened, hoping that my father could take care of me. But though that day he bound and stopped the bleeding, no earthly father could have healed the wounded heart he later left behind.

That hurt cried out for the love of a heavenly Father.

No matter my age, I will always be His grateful little girl—trusting, dependent, and filled with faith in the arms that will never let me go.

Warmed by God's Love

by Malinda Fillingim,
Rome, Georgia

It was a long, hot season under the South Carolina sun.
I was serving as a summer missionary with migrant
workers who were scheduled to pick crops for two
months. I worked with the children, doing all kinds of
things with them while their parents painfully picked
the crops. The compound where these hardworking
folks lived was a fenced-in kennel type of dwelling. No
privacy, little hygiene, and only a dirt road for the children's playground.

I tried my best to tell these sweet Hispanic children
about God's love, how Jesus died for them, and how life
was precious. But it seemed a hard message to sell
amidst their poverty, their seeming lack of hope for a
bright future, and the overwhelming odds against their
future being anything different than working in the
fields. But I persevered. I learned Spanish. I gave out
clothing and food, and I helped the parents make a better summer for their children.

Puppet shows were a big hit. The parents delighted
in watching the shows just as much as the children did!
The heat and poverty became invisible as we grew to
understand one another and appreciate the fellowship
we shared. But every evening I left the compound and
returned to the air-conditioned, nicely furnished room

where I lived. I had running water, a private bath, a nice bed, a car that ran well, all the food I wanted, and a future that did not include poverty or a nomadic lifestyle. I lived in two different worlds, one by day and one by night. I had an escape route. Did they?

As I contemplated my role in combating poverty, in helping to transform lives for God's glory, I began to wonder if I was making any difference at all. What good was teaching a few songs, a Bible story, a few educational sessions?

The week before the people to whom I ministered were scheduled to move "up north," Maria came to me with a special request. She was worried that her children would get cold as they traveled north and lived in colder climates. Did I have a blanket to give her? One that was soft and could keep her three children warm at night as they cuddled together on the floor?

I searched local churches, but blankets were not available during the summer. I didn't have enough money to buy one. So I reluctantly told Maria that I had not found a blanket. She cast her eyes down and thanked me for looking.

As I lay in bed that night, I felt the soft quilt that covered me. How I loved this quilt. I wanted it so badly and had worked many extra hours to buy it a few months earlier. It was a beautiful blue and white quilt, one with a simple pattern called "Wagon Wheel." It reminded me that life was a full circle, that we are all somehow connected to one another and to God. I felt safe under this quilt.

I began to wish I could get something just like this quilt for Maria and her children.

When I woke up the next morning, I instinctively knew what I should do. I folded my prized quilt, placed it in a trash bag, and put it in my trunk.

Maria opened it with great glee. "You give this to me?" she asked with appreciation and curiosity.

"Yes, I do, with great love."

"Yes, I see the love."

I still think about that quilt. I have never been able to afford another one. But I know that I am much richer because I allowed Maria to see my love, to know God's love, and to know how precious she is to God and me.

Quilts come and go, but God's love forever keeps us warm and safe.

Empty Arms, Full Heart

by Robin Brisbin,
Holly, Michigan

We had just learned we were expecting our fourth child, and I was not very happy about it. I had experienced very difficult pregnancies with my other babies and was sure this one would be the same.

As time went on, I noticed I did not feel the same. Something felt terribly strange. When I was twenty weeks along, my husband and I were on the east side of the state for business. That day I did not feel exactly right. The baby was moving abnormally, almost as if struggling for life. That was the last day I felt any movement.

I went in for my regular appointment a couple days later with my oldest daughter so she could hear the heartbeat. My worst fears were confirmed. My baby had died. I had to undergo ultrasounds and other tests for the next two hours. It was only by the grace of God that I did not break down. When we walked to our van, my daughter turned and asked, "Is our baby gone?" My heart broke. I said yes and then called my husband to tell him the news. Sobbing, I knew I needed to pull myself together for my daughter and get us home safely.

Many emotions began flowing through my mind. I wondered what I had done, or not done, to lose this baby. Did I not love it enough? What was God trying to show me? I was anxious for everything that lay ahead in the next few days.

I was to go through labor and delivery just as if I were having a live birth. There was no joy, no excitement, no happiness. Along with the physical pain would come an even greater pain in my heart. I remember my husband telling me, "I don't know what to feel because I am not as intimately involved as you right now."

He didn't realize how much he helped me by saying that. He expressed what many felt but could not put into words. He consoled me, hugged me, and showed his love by his support during the days before and after we had our little girl, Kelly Jo. I remember holding that tiny lifeless body in my hands for the first and last time.

The hardest part for me as a mother who had experienced the joy of having, holding, nurturing, and bringing home three other babies came when I left the hospital with empty arms. Every time I went to the store and heard a baby cry, I thought it should be mine. I would see other pregnant women and think it should be me carrying a baby right now. But through it all, God comforted me through His Word and through my prayers. He touched me in special ways, such as when a friend would send a card just when I needed the encouragement.

Six years have passed since we had Kelly Jo. My children know they have a sister who is in heaven with Jesus. After my dad and brother were killed in a car accident, my five-year-old said, "Just think, Mommy, Grandpa and Uncle Rick will be the first to see Kelly!" What precious words from this small child. She was clinging to the hope and assurance of seeing all of them again when we are reunited in heaven.

God has also given me the awesome privilege of

sharing my experience with others. Scripture reminds us that God uses these times "that we can comfort those in any trouble with the comfort we ourselves have received from God" (2 Corinthians 1:4). Friends sometimes tell me they have coworkers who just lost babies and wonder what they can do to help. I suggest they just love and comfort them by being there. Sometimes the quiet presence of a friend who truly cares is enough comfort.

I thank my heavenly Father for allowing me the opportunity to show others His love through the pain of empty arms comforted by His overflowing love that fills my heart.

Chapter Thirteen

Faith

We live by faith, not by sight.

2 Corinthians 5:7

Standing on Shaky Ground

by Michele Howe,
LaSalle, Michigan

Since the horrendous events on September 11, flags have proudly been displayed on homes, businesses, and automobiles. Patriotic apparel has been selling out in department stores. Pins, hats, socks, bumper stickers, music. . . all strike a solemn but proud note in the hearts of Americans as they ring up their purchases. More encouraging than these patriotic overtures are all the professions of faith in God. Billboards sport verses quoted from the Bible and my heart says, *Yes!* Magazine and newspaper articles reveal a dynamic resurgence in faith across our country. No economic, social, or educational corner in the United States remains untouched by these many and frequent declarations of belief.

Yet, there is a dark side to all this overt "religious coat-hanging." One evening I drove past a men's adult nightclub with its fluorescent sign sporting the words boldly and without shame, "In God We Trust." I could not believe my eyes. My stomach turned at the thought. Then righteous indignation took turns with outright anger. How dare such an establishment claim a trust in a Holy God. Their very existence relies on the opposite being true.

From morning until evening, any number of the Ten Commandants is broken within the walls of their building. It is amazing that such arrogant disregard for obedience to God's Word can be so freely and casually flaunted. Do those who don't truly understand the sacrifice made by Jesus Christ on the cross understand the price He paid on our behalf? Are we so naive we think that being a disciple of Christ requires nothing on our part? I wonder how many fellow Americans overtly embrace the comfort of religion but don't have the vaguest clue about what God expects of those who call upon His name. Our Holy God demands holiness. We are standing on shaky ground when we presume God's hand of blessing without first gaining His forgiveness.

Just as Christ died for us, we are likewise commanded to lay down our lives for others. In the same way that Jesus denied Himself, we are commanded to always consider our brother with higher esteem than ourselves. It seems that far too often, even we Christians who understand and embrace Christ's forgiveness live lives only overtly claiming His protection and power without sacrificing our desires, wants, and needs at His feet.

I confess that many times every day I ask God to bless our nation. I come before the throne of grace, begging God to forgive our nation for our frequent and flagrant sins against Him. For truly, when we envy, fight, kill, horde, turn a deaf ear, or simply become complacent, we Christians are no better than the owners of the men's nightclub who claim an inside track with God via a cheap fluorescent sign.

Our hope is in God; our trust should be in Him alone. But let us not be content with a mere outward show of faith. My prayer is that the Holy Spirit finds a home in every heart for eternity and that Christians become the hands and feet that will draw those without faith into the family. After all, we owe God everything, not just a sign in a window.

A Mustard Seed of Faith

by Bea Sheftel,
Manchester, Connecticut

We were in a small building in Willimantic, Connect-icut. Our friend had asked us to come visit her fellow-ship. It was called the Burning Bush Truth for Youth Ministry. The first thing I noticed was a poster on the wall with a man and woman. They had heart-shaped holes in their chests. The logo said, "God will fill the empty place in your heart."

Most of the others in the room were young like us. We sat on the floor to pray. Despite the lack of furni-ture, joy filled that room. I listened carefully as the min-ister spoke about God's love. A couple of people got up to tell us what God had done in their lives. Several were former drug addicts. I felt restless. I had been raised a Christian, but lately I had strayed from the path. We no longer went to church and rarely prayed.

The minister ended the service asking if anyone wished to have Jesus come into their heart. I lifted my hand. He prayed for all of us who raised our hands. The more he prayed, the more I felt as if a heavy burden had been lifted from my shoulders. I felt as if I could soar like a kite on a windy day. My husband and young son soon joined me in dedicating our lives to our Lord.

faith

At first, God's grace was sufficient. We had a period of respite in His arms as we went about our ordinary days with silly grins on our faces and happiness in our hearts. Problems, however, were on the horizon. My husband was out of work. He had two more weeks left on his unemployment after which we had no idea what we'd do. I claimed the promise of the Bible—if we gave to the Lord, He'd give back to us. So we sold our color TV set to make a donation to our fellowship.

After a day spent looking for work, my husband came home discouraged. I poured him a cup of tea and asked if he wanted to pray about it. At the kitchen table we held hands and prayed out loud. I said, "Lord, I have that mustard seed of faith You said could move mountains. Please move this mountain. Let my husband get a job so we can pay our bills."

After praying, I had the sudden urge to write down the kinds of jobs my husband liked doing. Pulling out a notebook, I asked him, "What type of work do you like?"

"I like to work outside," he said. I wrote that down. "What else?"

"I like to paint and work on lawns. I like driving and working with other men." My husband continued with all the kinds of things he enjoyed doing. As far as we knew, there was no job that incorporated all those things, but we prayed and looked to God for an answer.

Our other more immediate problem was groceries. After paying our rent and utilities, there was practically nothing left for food. Again I said, "Let's make a list and pray for the food we need."

My three-year-old son started the list off with peanut butter and jelly and a candy bar.

"Oh, Rob," I said, "a candy bar would be a nice treat, but the peanut butter and jelly is a good idea."

My husband said, "Write it down anyway. And put down a steak for me."

I laughed, thinking of practicalities, and said, "How about hamburger? I can stretch that for a number of meals."

He shrugged nonchalantly. "Okay, hamburger. Write down the steak anyway, and add a big bag of potatoes."

When it was my turn again I said, "Tuna fish is my favorite sandwich. So I need tuna fish and mayonnaise."

My husband pressed me. "Anything else?"

"Well. I'd love an eggplant, but that's a luxury."

He rolled his eyes. "God can give you an eggplant."

"Okay, okay," I said, writing it down.

We continued down our list with essentials such as bread, milk, cereal, and margarine. We added oil for cooking. I felt we should be practical in our requests so I added pasta. A pound of pasta could last us a week.

"I like cake," my son said.

"Me, too," added my husband.

This was turning into some list! I shook my head. "Come on. God promised to provide us with our daily bread, not luxury items," I reminded them. "We don't need cake."

But when they both protested, I lifted my hands in defeat. "Okay, I'll write down whatever you tell me." So the list went on. Mozzarella, tomato sauce, salad fixings. And then we prayed.

Two days later we came home from an evening of church fellowship to find bags of groceries on our front porch. I mean, bags and bags of groceries. Of course, we realized some kind soul from our church had brought the groceries. The ministry had probably paid for it. Even so, I looked at my husband in shock. "Who could have done this? Who knew we were desperate?"

He could only shrug. "We prayed. I guess God put it on someone's heart to help us."

When we looked in the first few bags, we found tuna fish, pasta, bread, hamburger, peanut butter, and jelly—all the practical items that any family could use to get through two or more weeks. But it was the other bags that had us hugging each other and crying our thanks to the Lord.

In the other bags we found an eggplant, several jars of tomato sauce, and mozzarella cheese. There was the biggest chocolate bar I'd ever seen, which had Rob dancing around the room. There was even a steak and a bottle of Worcestershire sauce.

"Can you believe it?" My husband laughed. "I forgot to pray for the Worcestershire sauce, but that's what I like on my steak."

My heart pounded. How good the Lord was to us. Tears rolled down my cheeks as we continued to pull out canned goods and frozen foods that would last more than a month. I sat down at the table and grabbed my husband's and son's hands.

"Let's pray our thanks." *God blessed us with plenty of food. Now we need to concentrate on employment.*

Every day my husband applied wherever there was an opening. He even left an application with the town hall although they had no posted openings. They told him they would keep his application active for six months.

It was only a week later, though, when he got a phone call from the town hall asking him to come in for an interview. We were so hopeful. This could be the answer to our prayers for his employment. A job with the town would be steady with vacation days, holidays, and health benefits. I waited impatiently for him to return from the interview.

By the broad smile on his face, I knew our prayers had been answered. "I'm going to work at the Parks Department. I'll be working outside. I'll have a truck to drive. Sometimes I'll mow; other times I'll paint."

"It's exactly as we prayed," I whispered in awe. He nodded. We hugged and danced around the kitchen, with Rob squeezing in between us.

One year later, my husband was made a permanent employee of the town. By then, we had saved enough money for a small down payment on a house. All our problems weren't over, but we knew the blessings of the Lord. We learned through this experience to trust in the power of prayer. God really did love us.

Our faith has been tested many times over the years, but each time we've reminded ourselves of all our answered prayers.

We know firsthand that a mustard seed of faith can move a mountain.

E-mail from God

by Linda Parker,
Windermere, Florida

I would like to think I always hear God's voice when He speaks to me, but the truth is, I've been known to miss it. Now and then, caught up in worry and earthbound timelines, I have simply failed to see His answers. Recognizing this, I sometimes whisper quietly, "Please, dear God, don't set fire to the shrubbery," lest He feel the need to get my attention through a burning bush. Goodness knows, as a working single mom, I have had enough problems keeping my yard tidy without the landscaping bursting into flames.

For many years I have supported my children by writing—stories, articles, advertising—whatever words I can sell. Writing gives a working mom a career pursuit from home, saves a small fortune in child care costs, and lightens the extra load of guilt that single mothers all seem to carry heavily upon their backs.

Besides, I love to write. I cannot "not write." The fact that people give me money to do it is both amazing to me and sometimes quite incidental.

This does not mean that the flow of money and the bills to be paid always come in synchronized harmony. My children were teenagers before I realized that they thought the words to the Twenty-third Psalm included, "Yea, though I walk through the valley of the shadow of debt."

And it was during one of these shadowy, wandering times, with writing assignments few and far between, that God might have resorted to E-mail to get my attention.

Four hundred sixty-four dollars. I needed it before the end of the month to pay the bills. Expenses were increasing, and my earnings struggled to keep up with my two growing girls, groceries, and an aging car.

So I did what writers do. I submitted outlines for books I thought were sure to be best-sellers and proposals for stories I thought would be "must reads." Editors did not share my enthusiasm. Before, in between, and around being a writer and a mom, I prayed.

I prayed, I stated my case, and sometimes I just downright begged. Was God hearing me? I questioned. Did He understand about compound interest and late fees? Time was running out, my faith was getting shaky, and I had overdue payments.

On the second week of that particularly uncertain month, I threw caution to the wind. I couldn't pay the utility bill, but I could sure spring for two Happy Meals after church and become one popular mom.

We ate our Sunday dinner on the playground. Then while my children squealed and giggled their way through a yellow plastic tunnel shaped like French fries, I spent a precious dollar and a half on the Sunday paper. My purpose: to search the want ads.

There it was! A job for a freelance writer! I'd never heard of the company, and I wasn't sure if I understood the job description, but I knew as I read the ad that I would apply as soon as I got home. As directed, I sent my resume to their E-mail address.

The next morning I checked my mailbox. "You've got mail." The company had sent me their seven-page application. Two days later, I had interviewed twice by phone, when Chris, my new editor in cyberspace, offered me the job.

We had discussed everything but my paycheck when Chris began to add numbers aloud. Would I submit two short articles each month for two hundred dollars apiece? Absolutely! Would it be all right if he sent my first payment in advance, and could I send him twenty-four articles this year? "Yes, yes, and yes," I answered, quickly realizing this meant an extra four hundred dollars per month. Just before hanging up, Chris added, "Oh, and you may have to do a little driving around for your interviews, so I am adding sixteen dollars per week to each month's check."

It wasn't until four days later when the check arrived that I bothered to do the math or comprehended that the sixteen dollars per week, for four weeks, brought the total of every monthly check to exactly four hundred sixty-four dollars. I grabbed my daughters and danced about the kitchen. *Why do I doubt?* I wondered. God, who loves me so, has always been there.

My children, quick to join any celebration, danced and hugged me back, glad to see their mother smiling again.

"Look," I said, holding up the check for their inspection. "God knew exactly how much money we needed to pay our bills. Aren't we blessed?"

"But didn't you get an E-mail about this, Mom?" Amanda asked.

I had no idea what my child could be talking about. She led me to the computer—and there it was. Two full weeks of almost daily communications with my new editor. I had studied their content carefully and responded promptly, trying to do my best job. I had missed one obvious fact.

"See, Mommy," Amanda said, pointing to my computer mailbox.

My new editor had casually mentioned to me that he pronounced his name "Chris" but spelled it in the traditional Greek way, with a silent "T" on the end. How typical that I had been too absorbed in worries to notice ten transmissions headings clearly marked, "To Linda, from Christ."

Prayers are answered, not in our time, but in His. And always at the right time. Our charge is to live in faith. Not to beg, but to believe.

Chapter Fourteen

God's Promise

The LORD will keep you from all harm—
he will watch over your life;
the LORD will watch over your coming and going
both now and forevermore.

Psalm 121:7–8

Milk Money

by Jo Upton,
Jonesboro, Georgia

No one could ever say my dad was a slacker. As soon as he finished his time in the navy, he went right to work loading airplanes for a major airline in our area. He and Mom were married before he turned twenty, and within ten years he was supporting a family of five on a tight budget.

As children we never felt deprived, because this was the '50s, a much simpler time. People didn't wear designer clothes or hundred-dollar shoes, at least not in the little neighborhood where we lived. My two younger sisters and I wore homemade dresses and worked hard to take care of our "school shoes," making sure they lasted until spring. That was when Dad bought our Easter shoes, the only other pair we would get for the year.

Mom and Dad worked as a team, because without living wisely, we couldn't have made it. Dad always worked overtime when it was offered and filled in for anyone taking sick leave or vacations. There were two things he was determined to give his family: a small but comfortable home, and regular meals, something he made sure we never lacked. We had only one car, but there was never a question about having enough groceries.

Dad had grown up during the depression and sometimes having an egg or a cup of sugar was a luxury no one could afford. That may have been the reason he felt it was worth any price to make sure we had good, nutritious meals. He made it his top priority, using the two checks he received each month to buy groceries first. Then, when the money ran low (as it usually did), he didn't have to worry about his family going hungry.

This same caring nature carried over into making sure we had proper diets at school, too. He often did without things he needed himself to make sure we had money for hot lunches, and that my first grade sister had milk money. The younger children had a morning break each day and could buy a cup of milk for a snack. Dad felt it was important because she was a fragile child, often sick and on medications.

The abundance of medical bills sometimes caused money to be scarce at our house. Dad was a responsible man, never allowing any debt to accumulate. Because he paid on time and in full, a few unexpected doctor visits could quite literally leave him penniless.

It was during one of these extreme money shortages that we all learned a lesson about God's provision.

Dad worked the night shift, going to work just before midnight and arriving home the next morning before we left for school. It was his routine to give my sister the money for her milk as he kissed her good-bye. The milk cost three cents a cup, but sometimes those were the only three pennies he had in his pocket. Of course, he never let us know at the time it was his last bit of change; he would just dig into his pocket in an exaggerated way to make us giggle, then scoop out the three copper coins to place lovingly into the hand of my tiny sister. He was totally dependable; she knew every day she would have milk when it was served. It was one of those small gestures that make little girls feel secure and dads feel like heroes.

One morning, however, he left work, tired and defeated. There were a few days left until payday, and the money was gone. . .not nearly gone, but totally. The last straw was when he felt inside his pocket to assure himself that he had milk money but couldn't find any change. His spirit crumbled. The one thing he wanted more than anything was to provide for his family. How could he go home and tell his little daughter that she couldn't have milk with the other children because he didn't have three pennies?

His heart cried out to God for help that morning as he walked to his parked car. Within seconds, he felt impressed to look down at the ground below him. He did so almost involuntarily, and there on the pavement directly in his path was a gleaming dime! He reached down for it, giving thanks quietly, and tucked it deep inside his uniform pocket.

This would be milk money for the remainder of the week, enough to last until his next paycheck.

When Dad arrived home, there was an extra spring in his step and a glow to his countenance as he reached inside his pocket for milk money. My sister's eyes were wide with delight when he handed her a dime instead of the customary pennies and told her to pay for the rest of the week in advance.

At just the right time, God the Father had given my dad exactly what he needed to provide for his child. He knew, and we later learned, that we had experienced a true-life miracle.

My Anthill Mountain

by Laura L. Smith,
Oxford, Ohio

My husband and I were breathing the clear, fresh seventy-five-degree autumn air in the sun-filled yard of our first home. We were planting tulip bulbs, which would sleep all winter in the red Georgia clay and bloom beautiful primary yellow and red in the first spring we would share as husband and wife. Armed with shovels, spades, and potting soil, we dug into our first yard project together.

We were newlyweds who had just moved with all our wedding gifts, transforming this empty building into our dream home. The towels, dishes, and sheets matched the wallpapers and paints we had selected, just as our hearts seemed to perfectly complement one another. We were living in a fairy tale.

"Ow! I've been stung by—*Jack!*" I jumped up from where I was kneeling and saw teams of dark red fire ants, the kind you can find only south of the Mason-Dixon Line, swarming up and down my legs.

"Are you okay?" Jack saw me swatting and dancing as I frantically tried to get these pests off. He joined me in swishing clumps of bugs to the ground.

The little girl who still lived somewhere inside me was grossed out by the hundreds of insects that had touched me. Honestly, it hadn't hurt that much, no more than a bee sting, but this was disgusting! I stood there dumbly, waiting for Jack to save me.

"Are you okay?" he asked again, half laughing at my pathetic reaction.

"I am, but *oooh!*"

"Why don't you go inside and get cleaned up?" he said and smiled. "I'll finish up here and be inside to check on you in a little bit."

"Thanks, honey," I said and kissed Jack and ran toward the front door. This was the out I was looking for. The ants had definitely ended my reverie of yard work, at least for today. As the shower heated up, I tugged the dirty shorts and T-shirt off and pulled the baseball cap off of my hair. Then I jumped into the water. Relief—warm, wet, soap, steam—the ants and the tenseness that had come with them seemed to wash right down the drain.

Maybe the water was too hot, or maybe it had been too long since I'd had something to eat, but I began to feel faint. Although I hated to leave the magic of my shower, I turned off the water, grabbed a towel, and stumbled to our bed. Closing my eyes on our pillows, my head began to clear. But how strange; my lips seemed swollen, like I had two fat lips. I rolled over to climb out of bed so I could look at my mouth in the mirror. But when my feet hit the floor my legs didn't support my weight. I collapsed.

I tried to pull myself up but couldn't even sit. Helpless, confused, and dizzy, I lay there wondering what to do next. I lost sense of time, but I thought Jack would be coming upstairs soon. If I could get over to the window to call to him, he could make sense of this. I managed to drag my body with the meager strength I found in my arms to our window. I couldn't raise my head high enough to see Jack, but I pounded my fist against the pane. Again, I lifted my arm just enough to bang on the glass. Could he hear me? Panicking now, as I was losing total control of my body and my consciousness, I gathered up enough might to flail one last time in hopes of getting my husband's attention. Everything familiar suddenly faded until I heard Jack's voice.

"Honey! Are you all right?" His usually calm voice was full of fear.

I couldn't respond. My lips and throat were so swollen they couldn't form words. I can't imagine what I looked like to him—limp on our bedroom floor, wet, tangled hair, puffy mouth, and unable to speak. Such a vision would have scared me, too. But I had no focus for thoughts, only comfort in Jack's presence.

"Okay." His logical brain was kicking into gear now. "We need to get you dressed and to the hospital. Okay? Okay." Jack answered for me. He kept speaking to me as he robed me in whatever clothes he could find and carried my deadweight body down the stairs and into the garage.

"I'm going to need your help," he sweetly pleaded, as he hoisted me into the backseat of our Jeep. I wanted to help, but I couldn't move a muscle, not even to put my arms around his neck or let him know I understood what he was saying.

We live five minutes from the hospital, but the first few seconds in the car are all that I remember.

"Hang on for me, kiddo," Jack whispered. We both were scared. I wanted to hang on, whatever that meant. But it seemed too hard. It would be much easier just to close my eyes and drift off.

I don't know how much time passed, but at some point Jack was talking to someone else. I couldn't make out either person's words, but I didn't care. My body was being moved; there must have been wheels involved. I heard squeaks and the rush of air. I wanted to be left alone to my deep slumber. More voices, antiseptic smells, cold steel on my back. Panic filled the air and suppressed even the distinct odors and sounds of a hospital. I could vaguely feel the chill of metal scissor blades against my skin as someone cut off my clothes. Pricks and tugs as an IV was inserted in my hand, a blood pressure monitor wrapped around my arm, and something to track my pulse was fitted over my index finger.

"One, two, three," someone shouted as chargers were placed on my chest. I should have been petrified by the implications of this swarm of physicians and nurses. But I couldn't open my eyes to look at them. I couldn't question what was going on, process what these actions meant, or even ponder if I would survive. All I could do was register the actual events as they took place, and then only as if they were happening to someone else—as if I were watching an episode of *ER* on television.

"Blood pressure 20 over 10! Let's go again, on one, two, three!" Again the shock that wasn't all that electrifying coursed through my limp frame.

At some point things settled down. Fewer people were in my room. Some of the panic had subsided. As my thoughts began to form for the first time since I had pounded on the window, my first one was, "Jack!" At least I tried to call out his name. He could sense it. I soon felt his warm hand on mine.

"I'm here. It's all right. You're going to be okay," he assured me with a whisper.

I was okay. I lived. I did not cave into the irresistible urge to shut out my senses and surrender to the peaceful darkness. My time, as they say, had not come. God gave me a second chance.

I had suffered an anaphylactic reaction. I was so severely allergic to fire ants that their venom caused my throat to swell shut, stopping air from going to my lungs and eventually to my brain. My ant bites could have been fatal. If Jack had waited even two more minutes, I would have died.

That would have been the end to our dreams for the future and to our perfect new life together. I would never have seen the tulips bloom. There wouldn't be any anniversaries, trips to Europe, or children. There wouldn't be any "us," just Jack alone in our new house with so many wedding gifts still unwrapped—alone with our unfulfilled dreams.

I was released from the hospital the next day and had enough strength to return to work the next week. I went through intense allergy testing and was armed with pills, shots, orders to stay out of the grass, and a Medic Alert bracelet in case a fire ant ever crossed my path again.

Life resumed. But things did not go back to how they were. The job I had attacked so passionately in the past seemed less important. Did it really matter if I got to the office by 6:00 A.M. so I could complete piles of work before anyone else arrived? Or did it make more sense to eat breakfast with Jack at home, simply because I was alive and we could?

As we planned our upcoming vacation, it didn't seem to matter anymore where we stayed or what we would eat. It also didn't seem critical for me to be patched into Wednesday's conference call from my tropical retreat. I just wanted to spend quality time with my husband and with the beauty of God's creation.

And should we really wait to start our family so I could climb a few more rungs on the corporate ladder?

I could certainly step on an ant between now and then, and Jack traveled so frequently he could be in an accident. We were not, I had discovered, untouchable. Why risk never having children together so that I could be more established in my career?

My priorities did a 180-degree turn. God had spoken to me loudly, clearly. Although young, successful, and happy, I was not in control of my life. No matter how much Jack and I planned our futures, they weren't in our control. I realized it wasn't our goals and dreams that were important, but achieving and experiencing them together was. God's ever-powerful hand would guide us along His path for our lives.

It took awhile for my body to heal from this trauma. My mind will never completely mend, and I am glad. The mental scars will hopefully continue to heal.

This event in my life was a blessing. God reminds me of the precious gifts He gives me every week when I go to my allergist for a shot and every morning when I fasten my watch around my wrist, next to my Medic Alert bracelet. So few are given a glimpse of how quickly their lives could change or what would happen if their lives ended abruptly. I had a near-death experience. I was able to see clearly for a moment the things in life that are truly important. I am determined to remember what God taught me that fall day. A small anthill became my mountain. I am a better person because I climbed it and looked out from its peak.

The Name on the Card

by Ginger Plowman,
Opelika, Alabama

The table was deathly cold, as were the doctor's hands that were swiftly at work to remove the small life whose heart had only just begun to beat. The room was spinning, and vomit rose in my throat as the shame of what I was allowing him to do to my baby threatened to choke the life out of me as well. Although there was no sound, no verbal plea, I could still hear an ever-so-small voice calling out to me in my despair. What was it saying?

No, please don't. . . . Please don't. . . . Please don't.

But it was too late. The voice was gone, along with the tiny body. Oh, the shame, the guilt, the depression, and the total sense of despair that followed. How could I do such a selfish and wicked thing? *What kind of a human being am I?* I wanted to die.

As I staggered to the exit door of the clinic, I noticed a nurse filing a card in her drawer. I suppose it had my name and the information concerning my dead baby. *So, that's it,* I thought. *His entire life is on an index card that will remain shoved between the Es and the Gs in that cold metal filing cabinet.* What did the card say? Did it say if it was a boy or a girl?

No, I think I heard someone say that you can't tell that early. Call it women's intuition, but I believe it was a boy. I've learned since then that God knits the little ones together in their mothers' wombs, so I guess only He really knows.

I can picture the holy hands of God forming his features, forming his personality, forming his likes and dislikes. At the time, I didn't know that so I kept telling myself over and over that it didn't matter. But somehow I knew that it did matter. I knew that something that mattered so very much was written on a card instead of living, breathing, laughing, and loving.

The card would never tell about the expression on his face when he takes his first steps or when he pedals a bike for the first time without training wheels. I'll never get to slip into his room after he has gone to sleep and just hold his sleeping body in my arms or adore the way his messy hair looks when he wakes up in the morning. He'll never know what a butterfly kiss is or experience the sheer delight of Daddy arriving home from work. He'll never know the warmth and security of cuddling with his mama after his bath. No, the card will not tell these things because they will not come to pass.

The card. What if someone I know starts working at this clinic and sees my name in the files? Now I am even more ashamed. I am worried about my reputation when I have killed my own child. Oh, the shame of someone finding out.

That was twelve years ago. It's November. Each autumn, as I watch the leaves change colors and fall to their death, I am reminded of my ultimate fall, the day I paid to have my first child put to death. One counselor said it's like an onion. Each year another layer of guilt-stricken emotion would adapt, harden, and peel off, only to have a new, fresh layer to suffer through. I've cried through twelve burning layers so far.

Since that day in the clinic, I met a loving Savior. I'd

known about His forgiveness and thanked Him for it, but I never felt the redemption. I knew it was there but I couldn't feel it. I'd cried out in anguish for Him to take the guilt and suffering from me, but there was no answer. Not until last night.

It was one of those dreams that seem so real. Every little detail is as though I am there. I am in the clinic, shamefully watching the nurse file away my card. The devouring darkness is like a heavy blanket wrapped around me so tightly that I gasp for air. Suddenly a man appears beside the nurse.

Oh, no. It's someone I recognize. Someone is going to find out what I have done. The man turns so I can see His face. No, please, not Him. . .anyone but Him. It's Jesus.

"Please go," I plead. "You shouldn't be here in this horrible place." But He doesn't leave. Instead, He gently takes the card from the nurse's hand. I begin to shake as I watch His eyes absorb the shameful reality of what I have done. Slowly, He drops His head and begins to weep. I am so ashamed that I have brought Him to this place for this reason. I hopelessly fall to the floor in despair.

I feel His hands on my shoulders, and I look up into His eyes, expecting His wrath. But I see no anger or condemnation, only compassion. His face reflects sorrow, and I am aware that it runs deeper than my own. He wraps His arms around me, and I bury my face in His chest. I weep harder. Our tears seem to flow in unison.

When I finally let go, He begins to write something on the card. I look down and find that He has written over my sin with His own name. He has written in a thick crimson red that is so dark and so rich that I can no longer read what was there before. There, in His own blood, the name of Jesus Christ covered my sin. The heavy blanket is lifted, and as I look back up into His holy eyes, He smiles the most tender smile as He whispers to me. . .

"It is finished."

Yes, it is finished. At long last I understand. There is no condemnation for those who are in Christ, only redemption. Let the redeemed of the Lord say so. I'm redeemed. I'm redeemed, praise the Lord!

Chapter Fifteen

Prayer

"Therefore I tell you,
whatever you ask for in prayer,
believe that you have received it,
and it will be yours."

Mark 11:24

Christmas Bear

by Timothy Michael Ricke,
Casselberry, Florida

It was a cold winter day as eight-year-old Mike ran home from school filled with great excitement. In just two weeks, the annual holiday festival at his school, St. Alexis, would begin. He ran in the front door with a swirl of leaves flying behind him.

"Mom, Mom, can we go to the holiday festival? I want to win the big Christmas bear for Dawn; she'd really like it, don't you think?" He was so excited. His mother smiled and nodded her head in agreement.

Dawn, Mike's little sister, had been bedridden for months with rheumatic fever. Somehow she wore a smile whenever Mike entered the room. She was always so pleased to hear his happy voice. Every day he told her that she was going to get better. Knowing what the odds might be of winning the treasured bear, his mom said, "We can all go to the festival, but let's not discuss the bear with Dawn. We'll make it a surprise, okay?" Mike agreed.

The holiday festival coincided with the first snowfall of the season, adding to the beauty and excitement of the evening for the children. The school band filled the night air with Christmas music. Mike was caught up in the wonder of it all. When he arrived at the school gym, he couldn't wait to "go fish" for the Christmas bear.

He reached deep into his jeans and pulled out the dollar he had earned over the last four months. He gave it to Sister Marie in exchange for a ticket and a plastic fishing pole and seventy-five cents back. Running over to the game, he swung the pole over the curtain. He quickly reeled in a plastic circle with a number on it. He was puzzled when Sister Martha said, "Michael, go over to that table and give them the circle, and they will give you your prize." She pointed across the room. He quickly ran over to trade his circle for what he thought would be the Christmas bear. His smile vanished as they handed him a noisemaker.

Quickly, he exchanged another ticket and went over the curtain again. He repeated the process until he was out of tickets. Thoroughly disillusioned, he quietly handed back his pole and walked over to his coat, slipped it on, and went outside to sit on the swing by himself. He swung back and forth, drawing lines in the snow with his boots.

That's where his mother found him. "Michael, sometimes things don't always work out for us, and we are disappointed," she gently told him.

He looked up into her eyes and said, "I know, Mom, but I really wanted Dawn to have that bear for Christmas."

"Well, sweetheart," she suggested, "maybe if you pray and believe, perhaps God will help you find a way to have something for your sister this Christmas." Then she repeated her renowned quotation. "Remember when God closes one door, He leaves another open." Mike shook off the sadness and smiled up at her.

At church that Sunday Mike quietly prayed, "God, would You show me a way to get a present for my little sister? She's been awful sick, and it would really make her feel better." He left church with great faith, believing his prayer would be answered.

On Monday morning, Father Cowth visited each class as usual but ended his morning message with a surprise. "Children, we are going to have a raffle. The money raised will be used to help the poor in our congregation have a joyful Christmas. Children, each ticket sold will be an entry for the contest. The grand prize will be the one item that was not won at the festival, the Christmas bear. The drawing will be on the last day of school before the Christmas break, December 20. But, remember, the winner must be present to win." Mike could hardly contain his joy.

Mike made a dash for home. "Mom! Mom! No one won the Christmas bear, and we're going to have a new contest for it!" he shouted with bliss as he burst through the kitchen door. He then proceeded to tell her about the contest and how the bear could be won.

"Well, Michael, looks like you'd better get busy!" she said with assurance in her voice. Away he flew. He canvassed the neighborhood as much as he could and then went downtown to the stores on Main Street. He put his heart and soul into it.

December arrived and Mike had sold only four tickets. His friend Ralph had sold one hundred four tickets through his father's hardware store, which didn't seem fair to Mike, but he did not give up hope. He just prayed over and over again, "Please let me win the Christmas bear for my sister."

He went to bed early the night before the drawing, totally prayed out.

Finally, after hours of prayers and waiting, the moment had arrived. The children assembled in the gym and waited as Father Cowth shook up the box of entries. He reached slowly into the box with eyes closed and pulled out the cherished ticket. He smiled as he looked upon the entry. "Okay, children, the winning name is Ralph McGuire. Ralph, come up and get your bear!" Father was delighted because Ralph's family had been very generous to the church, and it only seemed fair.

Mike was close to tears with disappointment and hurt. *I worked so hard and prayed and prayed,* he said to himself.

Once again Father Cowth's voice announced Ralph's name. "Where is Ralph McGuire?" he asked, looking over toward the sisters. Sister Maria told him that Ralph was ill that day. She also reminded Father that the rules required the winner to be present.

"Yes, that's correct, Sister, thank you." So he reached into the box to draw another ticket.

At this point, Mike was so busy feeling sorry for himself he wasn't paying any attention to what was going on anymore. It confused him when he felt hands patting him on the back and his classmates cheering over and over. "Way to go, Mike!" "Go get it, Mike!"

He'd won! He ran to the front with tears of joy filling his eyes, thinking to himself, *Wow, prayers do work!*

Christmas 1949 was a memorable one. Dawn received her Christmas bear, much to Mike's joy. She also regained her health.

Mike grew up with great faith and hope. To this day, he credits that event with his positive attitude. He's never stopped praying.

All the Pianos

by Lindy Johnson,
Isanti, Minnesota

I had to sell my sixteen-year-old daughter Paula's piano two years earlier. Now she was hoping there was a way we could replace it. Even a used one was out of the question. My four children and I were going through hard times.

I continued thinking, however, that a piano would provide an outlet for Paula's creativity and lift her heart out of depression. It had always worked before, and it was quite delightful to hear her original music flow off the ends of her fingertips. In times past, she would come home and play something that no one had heard before. It was always wonderful!

My heart swelled with the desire to give her a piano—and then sank with the reality of my financial condition. I turned to God, boldly, as I remembered the Scripture, "Delight yourself in the LORD and he will give you the desires of your heart" (Psalm 37:4).

I knew I could go to my Father God with this aching need to give my daughter a piano. I will never forget my prayer that day in 1981. I said, "Father, as Your daughter, I am asking You for a piano for my daughter. I have no money for it. Now I don't know how You will do this; I just know this is no big deal for You. You own them all. I only want one for Paula, so I am going to start looking in the newspaper in two weeks for Your blessing."

Only God could come up with the rest of the story. At the appointed time, I began looking in the newspaper for the blessing. What a feeling of adventure when I found an ad. I remember the trip across town to go look at the piano. I was prepared for whatever lesson I was to learn, but I had a history of answered prayer, so I was excited. The challenge was in the money. All I had was a twenty-dollar bill, and the piano was nearly nine times that amount.

As I drove to the appointment, my prayer was, "Well, Father, what do You have for me?" I could feel my heart bristling with excitement—like that of a little child. I was full of expectation because I knew that this was a godly heart's desire. God would do something—but what?

It was an old upright piano, in good shape. I gave the twenty dollars to her and said, "If I'm not back here within a week, then just figure I'm not coming back." She agreed to hold the piano for that long and gave me a receipt. I walked away wondering what God was going to do. It was definitely up to Him. For all practical purposes, I had just lost twenty dollars (no small amount to me in those days) if God did not "show up" with some money.

During that week, Paula's father arrived for his weekly visitation. I had not mentioned a word to him about the piano. You can imagine my thankfulness when he proceeded to tell me he had just received an unexpected IRS tax refund and then handed me exactly half of it. It was precisely ten dollars over the amount I needed to pay the balance on the piano! He could have kept the whole amount.

Paula was out of town with her church youth group on the day I arranged to have the piano moved. When she came home, she first squealed with delight and then was speechless. Ever so slowly, with her hands held up to her face, she walked over to it, as if tasting the moment. She sat down and barely touched the keys, as if touching a baby's face. It was such joy to hear her play again.

That piano enabled her to move forward with her music. Two years later, performing her own song, she took second place in the national church youth talent program. Now she is serving in her own music ministry in east Texas. Recently her ministry has shown evidence of branching out into other parts of the country to serve in churches that minister to the wounded.

This miracle of the piano continues to be a blessing—not only for Paula, but also for the many to whom she is ministering. Without it, she would never have come as far as she has. I am always reminded that God hears me and responds. God has a plan and I am blessed to watch it unfold.

A Woman's Journey

An Unexpected U-Turn

by Sandra McGarrity,
Chesapeake, Virginia

Finally, we were on our way! Pulling a heavily loaded U-Haul trailer behind our Duster, we left Florida and college days behind and headed north to the new church where my husband would serve as assistant pastor and school administrator.

We had packed that trailer full and still had to leave some of our belongings behind. However, our most precious treasures, our two little daughters, were safely tucked into the backseat. They were just as eager to begin this great adventure as we were.

We left early Saturday morning, planning and praying to arrive in time for a good night's sleep before joining the new congregation for Sunday morning services. Our only concern was our car, since we were pulling a heavy load. We had spent the last several years trying to keep the car going until Mike finished Bible college and we could afford to buy a better one. That car had given us a hard time, but it was still running.

We drove northward from Florida and were making good time through Georgia, when, just past the exit to Savannah, the car gave forth a shrieking, grinding noise and promptly rolled to a stop. Mike turned the key in the ignition several times, but the dear, old car refused to summon even a spark of activity. He got out and jiggled everything under the hood, then slid back into the driver's seat with the final verdict: The car was dead.

By this time, our daughters were close to tears, so Mike said, "We are obeying the Lord, and He has promised to take care of us, so let's ask Him to help." We all bowed our heads as he prayed, "Lord, I'm asking You to make the car start or show us what to do next."

When we raised our heads from prayer, we found ourselves looking into the face of a state trooper, bent down and peering into our car. The trooper took us back to the station in Savannah. From there, we called the pastor of the church to let him know that we wouldn't arrive on time.

It "just happened" that the state trooper's in-laws lived in Savannah. He called them to help us out. In a short time, they had picked us up and driven us to their home, helped Mike get a tow truck to bring our car and trailer to their house, and then fed us a steak dinner.

We spent the evening discussing our options, still not coming up with an answer. Since it was too late to do anything else, they insisted that we get some sleep and see what we could work out the next day. We gladly accepted their offer, grateful for the kindness of these strangers.

The next morning, our host asked that we join hands in prayer around the coffee table. He led in a simple prayer of faith that the Lord would provide. He then shared with us that his wife had a car that she had been trying to sell for months. Despite quite a bit of advertising and lowering the price several times, she had found it impossible to make the sale.

He handed us a receipt for the price of the car, made out to my husband. The notation at the bottom read: "A gift of love for the Lord's work." Our prayer had been answered.

Wanted: A Grandma to Pray

by Pastor John Roberts, Sterling, Colorado

I think it all started with the phone call from her granddaughter Sarah, the call that described what happened one day while the ten year old was delivering her paper route on her new bike. Her grandma's heart must nearly have burst to hear these words.

"Grandma Pinky, it was so scary at first. I looked up, and the big red car was coming straight at me. The next thing I knew, I was flying through the air, and I thought it would really hurt. But the big man came and picked me up and laid me down in the grass. My legs hurt where the car hit them, and my bike is smashed. But I'm okay."

That was no big man, thought Grandma. *That had to be an angel.*

Though Sarah could describe the "big man" very accurately, nobody else at the busy rush-hour scene had observed anyone matching his description. The policeman and the ambulance driver wouldn't call it a miracle, but they did say it was amazing. The huge dent in the front of the car would make anyone think someone had suffered serious injury.

So, having seen the hand of God extended on this occasion, Grandma Pinky made a decision, a love choice:

A Woman's Journey

"Whatever it takes, I'm going to pray for my grandbabies' safety."

Like most commitments that grandmas make out of a heart of love for their grandchildren, she probably didn't know everything it would involve. It didn't take long.

Sarah's paper route soon grew so much that her brothers joined her. Up every morning in the dark, they delivered huge loads of Des Moines' *Register* through the neighborhood—on foot. No more delivering by bike. The job required that they carefully place each paper against the front door of every house before 6:00 A.M. They had to get up at 4:00 and start on the route by 4:30 to get the job done.

That meant that Grandma was up at 4:00, too. Morning by gloomy morning, Sarah, Sam, Josh, and Jason bundled up papers in the predawn dark. At the same time, Grandma bundled them up in the arms of faith five hundred miles away, praying for God to protect them.

In a little while, the younger sisters, Bekah and Rachel, joined the early morning business, and all six of Grandma's Iowa grandchildren were getting up at 4:00 A.M., seven days a week, to pass papers in the dark.

Sometimes the early hours were pleasant for them, with singing birds accompanying their walk and budding roses perfuming their path. Other times, it was stormy or cold, with soaking rain or freezing wind to fend off. Over the years, several blizzards and a record-breaking flood made the job tough. Sometimes the neighborhood dogs snarled, and sometimes they slept.

But two things never changed. Every morning her six grandchildren got up to walk their routes. And every morning, Grandma got up with them, to pray them around the neighborhoods. In her heart's eye, she walked with them by faith, pleading the blood of Jesus for her babies from house to house, past barking dogs, across busy streets.

In the meantime, two more grandchildren came along in Indiana, and they, of course, were added to Grandma's list. Every step of every day in the lives of her precious ones came under the watchful care of her intercessory ministry. As others in her church learned of her early morning supplications, they asked to have their loved ones added to her list.

Soon she was praying for scores of families, doing spiritual battle over doctors' visits, baseball games, and school concerts of a hundred children or more.

Then one day, something unthinkable happened. A "postsurgical accident," they called it, which sounds so clean and sterile. It left Grandma in a coma, teetering between heaven and earth. The hands that were clasped so often in prayer lay limp by her sides. The head that bowed for years before God could now only rest listlessly on a pillow.

For two years she tarried, and the eight grandchildren for whom she had spent uncounted predawn hours before the Lord went frequently to the hospital room to pray for her. And then, she went home to heaven, leaving us full of blessing, but empty-hearted.

While we celebrate Grandma Pinky's presence with the Lord, there is a hole in the very fabric of our lives. Who will always remember our birthdays? Who will send us cards to celebrate our successes and console us in our crises? Who will make our favorite dessert at Thanksgiving? Who will lead us in singing "Happy Birthday, Jesus" over the phone on Christmas morning? Who will read the Easter story with us?

Most importantly, who will pray us through the

dark mornings of our fear? Who will hold us up before God as we tread the long paths of His service? Who will carry to God the heavy burdens of our lives?

The grandkids are all growing up now, and one of them has even joined Grandma in heaven. But, really, we're all still just babies. And we still need a grandma to pray for us. Is there anyone out there who will pray for the grandchildren?

My Secret Sanctuary

by Charlotte Adelsperger,
Overland Park, Kansas

This story first appeared in Stories of God's Abundance *for a More Joyful Life compiled by Kathy Collard Miller, Starburst Publishers, 1999.*

In 1966 I drove home from another discouraging doctor's appointment. A flood of painful emotion tightened my chest. "Why can't I have a baby?" I cried out to God. "All those tests—the pain and waiting have gone on too long!" I longed for a private place to let loose and cry. I passed St. Andrew's Episcopal Church in Kansas City. I felt drawn to go in, but practical thinking held me back. I could pray at my own church or in my own living room. Why go here?

Before I realized it, I had turned into the church parking lot. My legs felt heavy as I walked cautiously into the building. I slipped into a pew and absorbed the beauty of the sanctuary. To my relief, I was alone. Only the Lord was with me. I knelt as I focused on the cross of Christ, my Lord and Savior. He would be my Listener, my Intercessor.

Silently, I told the Lord how much I wanted to be a mother, spilling out my fears and worries. Then I released them all into His care. A gentle peace flowed through me. I left the church with a lighter step. Somehow I knew

God had heard and cared. But the uncertain journey continued. I underwent more medical tests.

Still no pregnancy. My husband Bob's face revealed sadness. Yet he remained cheerful and gave me constant loving support. A year later in July, my doctor scheduled me for surgical studies in the hospital. Just a few days before I was to go in, I was reading on our back porch when a deep sense of God's presence swept over me. Like a personalized message, memorized Scripture came to me: "Trust in the LORD with all your heart and lean not on your own understanding" (Proverbs 3:5).

I was filled with incredible assurance that I would become a mother! I didn't know how I knew, but I knew it was true. *Yes, I'm going to be a mother!* I called to Bob as he was mowing the lawn.

"Hey, I've got to tell you something!"

He stopped and hurried to the porch.

"It may sound crazy, but I've just experienced the most wonderful peace from God. I believe with all my heart that God is hearing our prayers. It's like He's telling us we will be parents!"

Bob hugged me, but I knew he had doubts. Later that evening, I wrote down the date, July 22, 1967, along with notes about the experience and the Scripture. Prayerfully, I placed the paper in my Bible. It dawned on me that I had discovered another "sanctuary"—our screened-in back porch.

A few days later our pastor visited me in my hospital room before surgery. I told him about my experience. He responded with a prayer for Bob and me as "the couple who dares to dream." Unfortunately, the postsurgical reports gave me little hope for conceiving. That hurt. Hadn't God assured me of His promise?

Bob and I continued to pray in trust. Then a strange

thing happened. In September I noticed indications that I might be pregnant. *Is this one of those "false" pregnancies?* I wondered. A few weeks later I went to the doctor. After an examination and pregnancy test, he said, "Charlotte, I can't believe it, but you are pregnant!" He expressed hesitation about the months ahead, but I was awestruck and began to cry. "God is so good!" I blurted out.

Of course, Bob and I were elated to see how God was working in our lives. We thanked Him over and over. Every day I woke up with the wonderful realization: *I am going to be a mother!*

Many people, including Bob, prayed for the health of our baby and me. My doctor checked me often, but it was a smooth pregnancy. I shall never forget the morning of May 9, 1968, when I gave birth to a healthy baby girl, Karen Sue. I watched her delivery by mirror and burst into tears of joy. Even the doctor was excited. He told the nurses, "I'm going to carry the baby to the nursery myself."

When the doctor saw Bob, he held our daughter up. "Meet Karen Sue!" he said, beaming. When settled at home, Bob and I began praying in thanksgiving at Karen's crib each night. This began a pattern of praying as a couple that has continued through the years—another sanctuary in God's presence.

One day when Karen was about four months old, I drove past St. Andrew's Church. I wanted to take her in, but I felt awkward about it. Yet before I knew it, we were out of the car. I carried her into the empty, still sanctuary. I looked into Karen's little face as I held her to me.

"This is where I talked to God," I whispered. "Here is where I prayed to be able to have a baby." My throat tightened, and I choked out more words. "You see, God in all His love, heard me. He gave us you!" I kissed her cheek and with blurred eyes I looked at that same gold cross on the altar. "Thank You, O Lord, thank You! I praise You!"

As I ponder these answered prayers, I know God in His wisdom doesn't always give believers everything they want. But He does act in our lives in sovereign ways. Two years after Karen's arrival, I gave birth to our son, John. Again, Bob and I were thrilled at God's gift.

My "secret sanctuary" at a church in Kansas City holds precious memories, and God has provided more secret sanctuaries in my spiritual journey over the years. A favorite one is the "together sanctuary" Bob and I have found every time we join in prayer. God provides abundant creative places for us to seek Him and to find Him— when we seek Him with our whole hearts.

Chapter Sixteen

Thankfulness

Be joyful always; pray continually;
give thanks in all circumstances,
for this is God's will for you in Christ Jesus.

1 Thessalonians 5.16–18

The Right Hour

by Ruth Lerdal Cummings, Maple Plain, Minnesota

The page stared back at me, no black, no white, no letters, no words. . .just a large blur. *What's happening?* I thought. *Why can't I see?* I stepped back and once again looked at my book. Nothing changed. Just the meaningless blotch of black and white fused into nothingness.

I called my ophthalmologist right away, who told me to come in first thing the next morning. Nothing had changed during the night, so at 9 A.M. I took the Greyhound to Wayzata. From there, I would catch the bus into Minneapolis.

I had to cross the street and walk two blocks to get to the bus in Minneapolis. Cars, vans, and trucks sped in front of me. I heard them but could only see them as a gray blur. I stood on the corner, confused, panic-stricken, and alone. I must cross but what could I do? Somehow I must reach the other side. I must get to the eye doctor.

What was it Jesus said about the end of the world? "And lo, I am with you always, even to the end of the age" (Matthew 28:20 NKJV). I would pray. The sound of speeding cars filled my ears, the warmth of the summer's sun touched my being, and the spirit of hope filled my heart as I prayed. *Please, God, help me get to that office. I need to get there.*

I heard no swish of angels' wings or the melody of

angels' songs, but I did hear a voice beside me. "Why, hello, Ruth. Is there a problem? Could I be of help?"

"Yes, yes, please," I answered. It was my neighbor Mandy, whom I had known for years. "I'm having trouble with my eyesight. I must make it to the doctor's office but can't see to cross the street," I said.

"Here, let me take your arm," came her reply.

She walked with me to the metro bus stop. She chatted about the day and weather and asked no questions. That was a welcome relief as I did not feel like talking. I was too worried about what was happening to my eyesight.

The ophthalmologist examined me and discovered I had experienced a homograph. Some months earlier, I had a corneal transplant on my left eye. Now my body had decided to reject the transplant. That explained why my vision blurred. Only the day before I had lived as an unafraid, in-control, full-sighted person. That morning, without the aid of a Seeing Eye dog or cane, I was more than a little afraid by my visual impairment.

My eye was treated, and my sight eventually returned. Many times, I think back to that day and Mandy's sudden appearance and helpfulness. It was too coincidental that Mandy came to my side at that moment. She had been my gift from God. The ability to call out to a Navigator who will direct our paths is available all the time, not just in our times of serious need. It is a lesson I cling to still. I thank God that He will always be with me as He was on that day.

Celebrate the Gift

by Eunice Loecher,
Woodruff, Wisconsin

It was early, not yet seven in the morning, the highway empty, except for an eighteen-wheeler. That's when I heard the voice, tempting, encouraging, "Go ahead, roll out in front of that oncoming truck. I promise no one else will be hurt, not even the driver. Everyone will believe it's an accident. You know you can't handle all this suffering and death. Take your foot off the brake, *now.*"

I released the brake and started to roll into the path of the truck. "No!" I shouted. "My family deserves better than this." My foot returned to the brake as the truck roared past. I watched the truck until it disappeared from view. My opportunity for escape, gone.

Two weeks earlier, my dad had received a terminal cancer diagnosis. That same week a doctor discovered my husband's colon cancer. His surgery had taken place late the previous day. I spent time in a hospital waiting room filled with prayers and hope. When the doctor came to talk with me, all hope died. My husband's cancer had spread.

Returning home later, I faced our children and comforted them as best I could. Then, I spent a sleepless night, my soul in anguish. So, here I sat at the end of our driveway. My husband, unaware of the diagnosis, needed to be told. My father and my husband, both dying, and no one else to care for them.

Courage. The word became reality as I watched my father and husband face the final year of their lives. Dad spent hours in the hospital receiving blood transfusions and fighting pneumonia and high fevers. Every day became a battleground for his life. Then came the final hospital stay. The staff politely told us, "Don't bring him back. There is nothing more we can do." We brought my father—my friend—home to die, and I began caring for him as I would one of my grandchildren.

When I think of that final year, one moment stands out as my lowest point. During the night, Dad had a seizure, and I thought he had died. Exhausted, Mom became ill with shingles and was unable to get out of bed without my help. My husband tried to help me that morning, but the chemotherapy had made him so ill he was in the bathroom vomiting. At that moment my daughter arrived with my six-week-old grandson. She was returning to work after her maternity leave. I was her only option for child care.

I remember standing in the living room holding that precious baby while crying, and yes, I literally cried out, "My God, my God, why have You forsaken me?"

Step by step, the Lord led me through those months. Mom spent a few days in the hospital recovering. Dad was moved to a rehabilitation center for a week and then was moved to our home.

On a warm, sunny August morning, Dad arrived by ambulance. Two attendants were moving the gurney toward the house as I came out to meet him. His eyes were closed. Sunlight bathed his face in its warmth. It came then, a smile of pure joy. Joy in the homecoming. A smile I would never forget.

Mom awaited his arrival in the bedroom I had prepared. She leaned down and took Dad's face in her hands
and began kissing him, murmuring words of love. I left
them alone together. Throughout the rest of the day, each
time I entered the room, Mom would be stroking Dad's
hand or kissing his cheek. Each night she went home to
rest, returning the next morning to her bedside post.
Love and devotion lasting nearly sixty years. Lessons for
the caregiver. Blessings for a daughter's heart.

I continued to care for my grandchildren every
day, a three-year-old granddaughter and a two-month-
old grandson. I would lay my grandson on Dad's bed.
Smiling, he would gently stroke the baby's arm or leg con-
tentedly. Such a short time for great-grandfather and
great-grandson to bond. Psalm 51, the second half of
verse 12, became this caregiver's constant prayer. "Grant
me a willing spirit, to sustain me."

Dad's final days went quickly, without suffering.
During the night that he died, I sat holding his hand.
My turn to tell him how much he was loved. He left me
peacefully to meet his Lord and Savior face-to-face.

Training. Preparation. My husband's death followed a
few months later. Each time a wave of grief washed over
me, the words "Celebrate the gift" came with it. I felt as
though God was shouting those words over and over
again in my ear, victoriously, triumphantly. "Celebrate
the gift!"

Immediately, my mind would flood with wonderful
memories, memories that replaced the numbing sorrow.
My husband had truly been God's gift to me. Over thirty
years of incredible memories. "Celebrate the gift!"

I began to realize God had a deeper message for my
heart. The questions came. Had I ever really mourned
the suffering and death of Christ? My answer: "No."

Each Easter I simply celebrated the gift, God's promise of eternal life, a promise of resurrection. These are the gifts that bring peace to my pain and hope to my heart. Gifts that I cling to.

I continue each day to celebrate the many gifts God brings into my life. The wonderful relationship evolving between my eighty-nine-year-old mother and me. We spend time together each day, first as mother and daughter and now as friends. We share the common experience of widowhood. All these parts bind us together in a unique way.

My youngest daughter took a leave of absence from her job while her father was ill. She came willingly to help me care for him at home during his final weeks. A bond of understanding exists because of what we endured together. We are able to celebrate this special gift of love we shared for a husband and father.

My gifts come quietly in sunrises and sunsets. Occasionally, they are a mixture of joy and sadness as with my grandson's first birthday. My husband and father lived to celebrate his birth, but neither of them lived to celebrate his first birthday. The gifts surprise me with the joy they bring as I witness my grandson's first steps, or the day my granddaughter lost her first tooth.

Most precious of all, the whispered promise, "Celebrate the Gift." Now, one day at a time, I'm learning to do just that. "The gift of God is eternal life in Christ Jesus our Lord" (Romans 6:23 NKJV). It is a gift for which I am more than thankful.

Valentine Dance

by Nancy Bayless,
San Diego, California

The brilliant red, heart-shaped box of chocolates on the shelf made me smile. Precious man. He remembered.

I turned in our bunk. My husband, Lynn, curled in a fetal position, slept beside me. Looking at his fragile body, I knew we would not be going to our annual yacht club Valentine dance. Sadness blanketed me. Cancer had squelched our dancing date.

I slid across Lynn and climbed out of our bunk. Gentle rain fell on the deck of our floating home, a thirty-six-foot trawler. Bleak mist hung over the sea and matched my mood of self-pity.

Pulling on clean sweats, I plugged in the coffeepot and stared out at the dismal day. Then my eyes swept across an array of Valentines gracing our dinette table. I leafed through them, feeling hugs and hearing giggles. Our combined families had remembered us in special ways.

"I love you big-time, Mom."

"Daddy, you're the only Valentine for me."

Hand-colored pictures of hearts from grandchildren and a red scribble on yellow lined paper from our towheaded, toddling great-granddaughter blurred my vision. *We are so blessed. Thank You, Lord.*

Carrying my cup of steaming coffee, I ambled up

the wet dock to get our *Wall Street Journal*. The rain had stopped and a chip of blue sky pushed through the clouds. At the head of the ramp, our yacht club ballroom resembled an art gallery of Valentines. Graduated hearts hung from the chandeliers. Red and white carnations embraced red candles, and perky red bows hugged the pillars. Longing consumed me. For twenty years we had whirled around this room, lost in the joy of the music and each other.

Our newspaper nested in the bushes by the front door. I pulled it out and walked back to our boat. As I climbed aboard, the sun broke through, shattering the gloom. Golden beams streaked the sea with subtle colors. On shore, a rainbow jumped from a tall pine tree and parachuted to oblivion. I turned on an oldie but goodie radio station. The strains of Glenn Miller's "Serenade in Blue" surrounded me with comforting familiarity. I put my right arm around my waist and held up my left arm. Then I danced all over our main cabin.

My spirits soared. When the song ended, I faced a plaque on our bulkhead.

"Forgetting those things which are behind and reaching forward to those things which are ahead, I press toward the goal for the prize of the upward call of God in Christ Jesus" (Philippians 3:13–14 NKJV).

Yes! I thought. *Yes!*

A fast, jitterbugging song, "In the Mood," blared from the radio. I peeked down at Lynn. He sat hunched on the edge of our bunk, his eager feet tapping in time to the music. I snuggled beside him. My arms crawled around his neck.

"Happy Valentine's Day! Thank you for the chocolates. Want to dance?"

He grinned at me. "Sure!"

Huddled together, our cheeks pressed against each other, our seasoned bodies entwined, and we rocked with the rhythm.

Acknowledgments

In volume one, I thanked virtually everyone I had ever known, so excited was I at having a decade-long dream become reality. When volume two arrived a few months later, I was pinching myself, still concerned about mentioning those who had given tirelessly of their time and talents to make a second volume possible. Today, as you hold volume three in your hands, I am numb. Numb with amazement that God could so richly bless me with this growing outreach ministry. Numb that He has brought into my life countless people to thank for helping this project grow into what it has become today. I trust each of you will know how important you are, even if your name is not mentioned, and how thankful I am for your ongoing support, encouragement, and love.

The phrase God Allows U-Turns truly does sum up my life. As a former "prodigal daughter," I can now see clearly how many times my heavenly Father was there to rescue me, guide me, and give me the wisdom to turn around in my tracks and retreat from ways destined to bring me to destruction. Today, I cannot imagine my life without God's love, without the knowledge that Jesus Christ died for me. I am a living, breathing example of how a life can be drastically changed. . .with God's help. I really am what the press has come to call: "The U-Turns Poster Girl."

The book you hold in your hands today is the third volume in a series of short-story collections that we know are encouraging and uplifting tens of thousands of people around the world.

And for that I graciously thank. . .

The thousands of author/contributors whose stories made us laugh, cry, and praise the Lord with joyful alleluias: You are gems beyond value. May God continue to shine His light on your lives.

My dearest husband, Kevin: Christ is my foundation, and you are the cornerstone of my life. Without you, success would not taste as sweet.

My son, Christopher: Outstretched arms are waiting for you. . .those of Jesus Christ and mine. It is never too late to make a U-turn. I miss you. I love you.

The special people in my life who show me often how God's love is all around us: Dolores Gappa, Cheryll Hutchings, Mandy Bottke, Kermit Bottke, Kyle Bottke, Lisa Copen, Debbye Butler, Linda Lagnada, Pastor Ron Wik, and Sharol Wik. A special thank-you to: Chip MacGregor, my publishing team at Barbour/Promise Press, the U-Turns Grassroots Promotional and

Volunteer Groups, Linda Evans Shepherd and the AWSA group of awesome ladies, Fred Littauer and Florence Littauer and my UpperCLASS ladies, Marita Littauer and all the amazing CLASS Instructors, Jennifer Johnson, Ramona Richards, and the hundreds of U-Turns contributors whose E-mails keep me encouraged and blessed on a daily basis.

Above all, I give praise and thanks to my Holy Father. His unconditional love and the plan He had for me even before I was born, helped me leave behind the ways of the world, ways that were leading me down paths of destruction, hitting one dead end after another. The Lord alone turned me around and set my path straight. Thank You, my most holy Lord, for giving me the wisdom to understand not only that God Allows U-Turns, but that no matter what I have done I can continue to turn my heart and mind toward You. You will always forgive me; You will always love me; You will always bring me the peace I need. Because it is so very true. . .God Allows U-Turns!

ALLISON

WE CAN ALL
CELEBRATE THE GIFT!

Dear reader, I can't leave without asking one most important question. Do you have a personal relationship with the eternal God? I'm not talking about "getting a religion." I'm talking about "getting a relationship." You may have read every word of this book and yet never experienced the peace and strength and hope that our authors have shared with you here.

I spent decades of my life looking for fulfillment in all the wrong places. Today, I have peace, strength, and hope because there was a time in my life when I accepted Jesus as my personal Savior. That is what I mean by getting a "relationship," not a "religion."

The way is simple: It only takes three steps.

- Admit that you are a sinner: "For all have sinned and fall short of the glory of God." Romans 3:23
- Believe that Jesus is God the Son and He paid the wages of your sin: "For the wages of sin is death [eternal separation from God], but the gift of God is eternal life in Christ Jesus our Lord." Romans 6:23
- Call upon God: "If you confess with your mouth, 'Jesus is Lord,' and believe in your heart that God raised him from the dead, you will be saved." Romans 10:9

Our Web site has a "Statement of Faith" page that you might find interesting and comforting. On that page you will find helpful (and hopeful) links to other spiritually uplifting Web pages. Please visit us at http://www.godallowsuturns.com.

Salvation is a very personal thing. It is between you and God. I cannot have faith enough for you; no one can. The decision is yours alone. Please know that this wonderful gift of hope and healing is available to you. You can Celebrate the Gift! You need only reach out and ask for it. It is never too late to make a U-turn toward God. . .no matter where you have been or what you have done. Please know that I am praying for you.

God's Peace and Protection Always,
ALLISON GAPPA BOTTKE

Future Volumes of
GOD ALLOWS U-TURNS

The stories you have read in this volume were submitted by readers just like you. From the very start of this inspiring book series, it has been our goal to encourage people from around the world to submit their slice-of-life, true short stories for publication.

God Allows U-Turns stories must touch the emotions and stir the heart. We are asking for well-written, personal, inspirational pieces showing how faith in God can inspire, encourage, heal, and give hope. We are looking for human-interest stories with a spiritual application, affirming ways in which Christian faith is expressed in everyday life.

Because of the huge response to our call for submissions, we plan to publish additional volumes in the U-Turns series every year.

Your true story can be from 300–1,500 words and must be told with drama, description, and dialogue. Our writer's guidelines are featured on our Web site, and we encourage you to read them carefully. Or send us an SASE for a copy of the guidelines. Please note the two addresses below.

To Request Guidelines:
GOD ALLOWS U-TURNS
P.O. Box 668 - DEPT. V3
Brunswick, OH 44212

Editorial Offices:
GOD ALLOWS U-TURNS
P.O. Box 717
Faribault, MN 55021-0717

E-mail: editor@godallowsuturns.com
http://www.godallowsuturns.com

Fees are paid for stories we publish, and we will be sure to credit you for your submission. Remember, our Web site is filled with up-to-date information about the book project. Additionally, you might want to take advantage of signing up to be on our free "Hotline Update" list for Internet users. For a list of current *God Allows U-Turns* books open to submissions, as well as related opportunities, visit us at:

http://www.godallowsuturns.com

SHARING THE SUCCESS:
THE GOD ALLOWS U-TURNS
FOUNDATION

One of the most profound lessons in the Bible is that of "Giving." The Holy Bible is quite clear in teaching us how we are to live our lives. Scripture refers to this often, and never has the need to share with others been so great.

"Give, and it will be given to you. A good measure, pressed down, shaken together and running over, will be poured into your lap. For with the measure you use, it will be measured to you" (Luke 6:38).

In keeping with the lessons taught us by the Lord our God, we are pleased to have the opportunity to donate a portion of the net profits of every *God Allows U-Turns* book to one or more nonprofit Christian charities. These donations are made through the GOD ALLOWS U-TURNS FOUNDATION, a funding mechanism established by Allison Gappa Bottke as a way to share the success of this growing U-Turns outreach ministry.

For details on the beneficiaries of the volume you are now holding, please visit our Web site at: http://www.godallowsuturns.com.

ABOUT OUR EDITORS

ALLISON GAPPA BOTTKE lives in southern Minnesota on a twenty-five-acre hobby farm with her entrepreneur husband, Kevin. She is a relatively "new" Christian, coming to the fold in 1989 as a result of a dramatic life "U-turn." The driving force behind the God Allows U-Turns Project, she has a growing passion to share with others the healing and hope offered by the Lord Jesus Christ. Allison has a wonderful ability to inspire and encourage audiences with her down-to-earth speaking style as she relates her personal testimony of how God orchestrated a dramatic U-turn in her life. Lovingly dubbed "The U-Turns Poster Girl," you can find out more about Allison by visiting her information pages on the book's Web site:

http://www.godallowsuturns.com/aboutauthor.htm
http://www.godallowsuturns.com/modeling.htm
http://www.godallowsuturns.com/gappabottke_speakerinfo.htm

CHERYLL MARIE HUTCHINGS was born in Ohio, where she has lived all her life. She and her family live in a rambling ranch home minutes from "civilization," yet secluded enough to enjoy the area wildlife that ambles through her own backyard in abundance. Cheryll and her husband, Robert, are raising two teenage sons, Aaron and Scott. In addition to her work as coeditor of the U-Turns project, Cheryll currently works for the Brunswick Community Recreation Center.

DEBBYE BUTLER joined the U-Turns team as an assistant editor with this volume. An award-winning former editor/writer for a Fortune 500 company, and cofounder and president of Circle City Singles, Inc., Debbye lives in Indianapolis, where she is actively involved with her church. A freelance writer and editor, Debbye works from her home, where she and her cat, Irma, live with oodles of Mary Engelbreit objets d'art and lots of warm and cozy knickknacks. Her hobbies include scuba diving, "dirt therapy," and eating chocolate—not always in that order.

CONTRIBUTING AUTHOR BIOS

CHARLOTTE ADELSPERGER has authored three books and written for more than seventy-five publications, including volumes one and two of *God Allows U-Turns*. Charlotte is a popular speaker to church groups and can be contacted at 11629 Riley, Overland Park, Kansas 66210. Phone: 913-345-1678.

NANCY BAYLESS resides in San Diego, California, where she is a seasoned writer. Her many articles have appeared in numerous Christian magazines and books.

ANGELA KEITH BENEDICT has been writing professionally since May of 1961 (*Leave it to Beaver*). She has written three books and been published in magazines for all ages. Angela is a church pianist.

MELANIE BOWDEN is a writer, postpartum doula, and mother of two. Her work has appeared in *Shape* magazine, *Writer's Digest*, United Parenting Publications, and others. She's currently working on a book titled *The Postpartum Family Plan*. Contact: melaniebowden@earthlink.net.

LANITA BRADLEY BOYD is a mother, grandmother, writer, volunteer, and former teacher living in Fort Thomas, Kentucky, with her husband, Steve. She enjoys walking, reading, traveling, church ministries, working with Steve, and being with her family.

ROBIN BRISBIN is a homemaker and freelance writer who enjoys helping in her children's classrooms, reading, and staying active in her local church. She and her husband, Ron, have four children and reside in Holly, Michigan.

LEONE A. BROWNING has over three hundred articles published in more than forty-five magazines. She enjoys fruitful days of writing at the age of eighty-two. Leone has been married for sixty-one years to a retired minister who also writes. Three great-grandchildren keep them in touch with today's world.

DEBBYE BUTLER is an award-winning former editor/writer for a Fortune 500 company, and cofounder and president of Circle City Singles, Inc. Her hobbies include scuba diving, "dirt therapy," and eating chocolate.

SANDRA J. CAMPBELL is a published author who resides in Garden City,

Michigan, with her husband, Michael. She is also thrilled to be one of the Three Ol' Bags, a trio of travel writers who visit, photograph, and write articles about places of interest in their Great Lake State. (www.threeolbags.com)

CANDACE CARTEEN has been writing since age eight. She is married to her best friend. They have one adopted son and are currently praying for a daughter to adopt.

JOAN CLAYTON is a retired elementary educator. She is currently writing her seventh book and has over four hundred articles published. She is presently the religion columnist for her local newspaper. Her husband, Emmitt, is God's gift to her for fifty-three years.

LISA COPEN is the founder of Rest Ministries, a nonprofit organization that serves people who live with chronic illness or pain. She is the author of several books and Bible studies for people who are chronically ill, a CLASS graduate speaker, and freelance writer. She lives in San Diego with her husband, Joel, where they do Web and sound design through their home-based business, JLC Productions. (www.restministries.org)

RUTH LERDAL CUMMINGS lives in the Midwest. God, family, and country are her loves, and writing her avocation. She and her husband, Gordon, find joy in their two daughters and six grandchildren. (rlcruth@mymailstation.com)

BARBARA CURTIS is an award-winning freelancer with two published books as well as five-hundred-plus published articles. Mother to twelve—including three adopted sons with Down's syndrome— Barbara holds a B.A. in Philosophy as well as an AMI Montessori teaching credential. Visit her at www.barbaracurtis.com.

KRIS DECKER lives with her husband, Dennis, and children Caitlin and Ryan in Blaine, Minnesota. She is a freelance writer, artist, and editor of *Esther,* a new E-magazine for women who long to be the person God wants them to be. Contact her at EstherEzine@aol.com.

EVA MARIE EVERSON is a contributing author to a number of publications. Her work includes *Shadow of Dreams, Summon the Shadows, True Love,* and *One True Vow.* For six years she taught Old Testament theology and currently speaks to churches and writer's groups across the country.

Contributing Author Bios

SUSAN FARR FAHNCKE is the author of *Angel's Legacy* and runs her own inspirational Web site, www.2theheart.com. She has stories in *God Allows U-Turns* volumes one and two and is excited to be a part of the series! E-mail Susan at Editor@2theheart.com.

MALINDA FILLINGIM is the associate pastor at Garden Lakes Baptist Church in Rome, Georgia. She hopes to get at least one of her children's books published, at least before her daughters Hope and Hannah have kids of their own! E-mail her at fillingim@roman.net.

RUSTY FISCHER is a popular Christian author whose stories have appeared in *Chicken Soup for the Soul* and *Cup of Comfort*. Rusty is a freelance writer who enjoys working at home—mostly because it allows him to spend more time with his beautiful wife, Martha.

BARBARA JEANNE FISHER resides in Fremont, Ohio. She has articles in national magazines, eleven *Chicken Soup for the Soul* books, and has published two children's books. Her first novel, *Stolen Moments*, fictionally portrays her own personal dealings with lupus. Her goal in writing is to use the feelings of her heart to touch the hearts of others.

KAREN L. GARRISON is an award-winning author whose stories appear in *Woman's World, Chicken Soup for the Soul,* and *God Allows U-Turns.* Inspired by her two young children, Abigail and Simeon, she is currently working on a children's book. A wife and mother, Karen describes her family life as the closest thing to "heaven on earth." You may reach her at INNHEAVEN@aol.com.

CAROL L. GENENGELS and her husband have three children and five grandsons. They live on scenic Hood Canal near Seattle. She is the cofounder/director of A Woman's Touch Ministry, and enjoys traveling, teaching, and prayer. Contact her at awtcarolg@juno.com.

NANCY B. GIBBS is a writer, pastor's wife, mother, and grandmother. Her stories have appeared in over thirty books and dozens of magazines including *Chicken Soup, Stories for the Heart, Heartwarmers, Guideposts Books, Woman's World,* and *Family Circle.* She may be contacted at Daiseydood@aol.com.

AMY GIVLER and her fellow-physician husband, Don, are raising three children in Monroe, Louisiana. A cancer survivor, her first book is for people newly diagnosed with cancer. "Please Forgive Me" first appeared in *Moody* magazine.

ANNE GOODRICH is a Web designer in Kalamazoo, Michigan, the very blessed mother of three beautiful children, and creator of OhAngel!com (www.ohangel.com), an inspirational E-card Web site.

ELIZABETH GRIFFIN resides in Edmonds, Washington, and is a wife and the mother of two young boys. She enjoys writing in her spare time.

DIANE GROSS lives in Warren Robins, Georgia, and is a mother of four, grandmother of four, and a published author and poet.

PATTY SMITH HALL is an active member of the American Christian Romance Writers and is currently seeking a publisher for her completed novel, *Tender Hearts*. She resides in Hiram, Georgia, with her husband, Dan, and their two daughters, Jennifer and Carly.

GAIL HAYES is an international speaker and writer. She had her first child at age forty-one and her second at age forty-three. She presently lives in Durham, North Carolina, with her husband, R. Douglas, and their two miracles, Joshua Matthew and Gabrielle Christina.

MARGARET HOFFMAN lives in Pennsylvania with her husband and three of their five children, ranging in age from thirteen to twenty-three. She has two grandchildren. Now in her fifteenth year of homeschooling, she has found it to be rewarding and humorous at times. Born and raised in Massachusetts, she spends a good bit of time at her grandparents' home on Harraseeket Bay in Maine. It was her grandmother who led her to the Lord at a young age.

MICHELE HOWE is a book reviewer for *Publishers Weekly, CBA Marketplace,* and *CCM Magazine.* She has published over six hundred articles and is the author of *Going It Alone: Meeting the Challenges of Being a Single Mom* and *Pilgrim Prayers for Single Moms.* She lives in LaSalle, Michigan, with her husband and four children. E-mail her at jhowe@toast.net.

MILDRED HUSSEY was rescued from an uncertain future at the mercy of an unloving father when she came to fully rely on a new relationship with her heavenly Father. God proved Himself a faithful Father. Today, almost seventy years later, she still walks in His love.

ELLEN JAVERNICK is a first grade teacher in Loveland, Colorado. She is the author of fifteen children's books and writes inspirationals for numerous magazines and anthologies. She enjoys playing tennis and spending time with her five children and their families. Ellen can be reached at javernicke@aol.com.

AMY JENKINS specializes in creative nonfiction and health writing. Visit her online at www.AnthologiesOnline.com and www.aThirdPerson. com. Look for her upcoming book *Bommin: Inside the Biggest Generation.*

LINDA LAMAR JEWELL, from Albuquerque, New Mexico, is a CLASS graduate, author, and workshop teacher. Her students learn to express themselves in journals, notes, and letters. She can be reached at linda@classervices.com. Visit www./lindajewell.html for a workshop listing, or contact craig@classervices.com or 505-899-4283 for booking arrangements.

JENNIFER JOHNSON lives in Minnesota where she is studying to become a registered nurse. With a passion for ministry to children, Jennifer looks forward to returning to Third World countries where she can share Christ's love.

LINDY JOHNSON is a published author, recently in *Decision,* December 2001 issue, and a member of the Minnesota Christian Writers Guild. She is writing a testimonial book, *Prayer—Why Pray Anyway?* She is also a songwriter/performer of Christian contemporary music.

LAROSE KARR lives in Sterling, Colorado, with her husband and four children. She enjoys ministering and speaking to women. She believes her writing is a gift from God and gives Him all the glory! Contact her at 181 Acoma St. Sterling, Colorado 80751, Phone: 970-526-2444, or E-mail: rosiebay@kci.net. Her stories appear in volumes one and two of *God Allows U-Turns.*

MAIE KELLERMAN was born and raised in southern Africa, and now lives with her family on the shores of Lake Huron in Canada. A chemical engineer by trade and a teacher by vocation, she finds purpose in life by trying to listen for God's purpose with her.

BRANDI LENTZ now resides in Renton, Washington, but grew up on a farm in Bellingham, Washington, where she lived next door to a tiny country church her family attended. In her U-turn back to Jesus Christ, she yearns for those childhood feelings in her quest of rebuilding her relationship with Him. Each time she drives past the still-standing church and sees this place in her history, her heart warms.

DELORES CHRISTIAN LIESNER enjoys looking at life through God's love and sense of humor. She turns everyday incidents into entertaining memories and opportunities to share the abundant life God promised in John 10:10. Delores considers being asked to share special occasion poetry, Devotions in a Box, PMS stories, and AGWC (A Grandma Who Cares) a "boomerang of joy." "You can never outgive the Lord!" says Dee. She can be contacted at godisgood@voyager.net.

EUNICE LOECHER is a full-time grandma and part-time writer. She lives in Woodruff, Wisconsin. Her stories appear in volumes one and two of *God Allows U-Turns*.

ALYSE A. LOUNSBERRY is a writer living in Florida. A former senior editor with Word Publishing and section editor for the *New York Times* newspaper chain, she writes to encourage and inspire Christian women.

SANDRA McGARRITY is the author of *Woody,* released in 2001 by America House Publishers. Her writing has appeared in *Virtue* and *Christian Reader* magazines. A native of Tennessee, she resides in Chesapeake, Virginia, with her husband of twenty-nine years. She has two grown daughters and one "son-in-love."

LYNN D. MORRISSEY is the editor of the best-selling *Seasons of a Woman's Heart* and *Treasures of a Woman's Heart* (Starburst), a contributing author to numerous best-sellers, and a CLASS staff member and speaker specializing in prayer-journaling and women's topics. Contact here at PO Box 50101, St. Louis, MO 63105. (words@brick.net)

CHERYL NORWOOD and her husband, Mike, live with their Siamese cat, Princess Jasmine, in their tiny castle north of Atlanta, Georgia. She has articles and stories in area newspapers and magazines, the *God Allow U-Turns* series, the *Heartwarmers* series, and in the 2002 devotional book, *Penned from the Heart.* She is president of the Cherokee Christian Writers Group.

KAREN O'CONNOR is an award-winning author, writing mentor, and popular speaker for church and professional events. She was named

Writer of the Year for 1997 by the San Diego Christian Writers Guild. For more information visit www.karenoconnor.com.

LINDA PARKER is an author and educator. Her most recent book, *A FabJob Guide to a Career as a Professional Golfer,* is currently available online at www.fabjob.com. She is a contributor to volumes one and two of the *God Allows U-Turns* series.

SHERYL PELLATIRO resides in Troy, Michigan, and is the founder and president of Solid Truth Ministries. (www.solidtruth.com)

GINGER PLOWMAN, wife and mother of two, is the author of *Wise Words for Moms* and founder of Preparing the Way Ministry, for which she speaks on biblical parenting from coast to coast. For more information visit her web site at www/gingerplowman.com.

MARK L. REDMOND has been a high school English teacher for twenty-five years and a freelance writer for twelve. He has written dozens of short stories and a series of books for middle-grade readers, *The Adventures of Arty Anderson.*

TIMOTHY MICHAEL RICKE is a photographer, writer, the Entrepreneur of the Year, and business coach. He resides in Orlando, Florida, and can be reached at www.timricke.siteblast.com.

PASTOR JOHN ROBERTS lives in Sterling, Colorado, where he is senior pastor at First Baptist Church in Sterling. He writes a weekly religious column for the local newspaper and has been previously published in volumes one and two of *God Allows U-Turns*. He and his wife, Debbie, have two children, David and Laura.

JULIE SAFFRIN lives in Excelsior, Minnesota. A freelance writer of numerous articles, she just finished *That Summer Place* and is at work on her second novel, *One Blood.* Say hi to Julie at www.home.talkcitycom/-BookmarkBlvd/juliesaffrin or e-mail ssja@qwest.net.

BEA SHEFTEL has been a freelance writer and editor for decades. She lives in Connecticut with her husband of thirty-seven years, her two dogs, and her son, Rob. She has two books of poetry, three romantic novellas, and hundreds of articles, short stories, and poems published in magazines and anthologies. Her memoir Web site receives thousands of hits every month www.memoirwritersonline.com. According to

Sheftel, her E-book, *The Writing Plan,* is a best-seller. (http://members.tripod.com/~Beawriter/report.html)

LINDA EVANS SHEPHERD, of Longmont, Colorado, is the mother of two and has been married for over twenty years. She is a nationally known speaker and founder of Winning Women (winningwomen. info), Advanced Writers and Speakers Association (awsawomen.com), and the host of Right to the Heart Radio (righttotheheart.com). Her latest books include *Teatime Stories for Women* (Honor). You may contact Linda at www.sheppro.com.

DEBBIE HANNAH SKINNER lives in Amarillo, Texas, with her husband and daughter. A public schoolteacher for fourteen years, she founded Mirror Ministries in 1997. Through this ministry, God has opened doors for her to communicate the hope found in Jesus Christ to women all over the world. Debbie weaves together words, watercolors (she's an artist), music, and teachings from Scripture as she speaks. Contact her at www.dhskinner.com.

LAURA L. SMITH grew up in Columbus, Ohio, graduated from Miami University in Oxford, Ohio, and worked for ten years for a shopping mall developer. Laura "retired" to pursue her dreams of motherhood and writing. She returned to Oxford where she now lives with her husband, daughter, and son.

GLORIA CASSITY STARGEL, assignment writer for *Guideposts* and freelance writer for *Decision* and others, is author of *The Healing—One Family's Victorious Struggle With Cancer,* an autobiographical story of faith, hope, and love. The book will encourage anyone facing cancer—and those who love that one. Visit www.brightmorning.com or call 1-800-888-9529.

ROSE SWEET (www.RoseSweet.org) is a speaker and author whose latest book, *A Woman's Guide to Healing the Heartbreak of Divorce* (Hendrickson 2001), helped inspire and encourage her niece, Kristin, after her broken romance.

JO UPTON is a freelance writer with more than fifteen years' experience. Her work has appeared in magazines, books, newsletters, and various Web sites. She is married, with four children and two grandchildren.

Contributing Author Bios

REVEREND MICHAEL F. WELMER has been in the parish ministry for thirty-eight years. He and his family reside in Houston, Texas, where he serves as senior pastor of Epiphany Lutheran Church. Pastor Welmer is a freelance writer.

BETTY WINSLOW, a writer and school librarian from Bowling Green, Ohio, loves reading, writing, singing, and spending time with her husband, children, and granddaughter, Kendall. She also loves to hear from her readers and can be contacted at freelancer@wcnet.org.

ALSO AVAILABLE FROM PROMISE PRESS

GOD ALLOWS U-TURNS
1-58660-300-0

MORE GOD ALLOWS U-TURNS
1-58660-301-9

COMING SOON. . .

GOD ALLOWS U-TURNS:
American Moments
1-58660-581-X

Paperback, 5"x8", $9.99

AVAILABLE WHEREVER BOOKS ARE SOLD
Or order from:

Barbour Publishing, Inc.
P.O. Box 719
Uhrichsville, OH 44683
www.barbourbooks.com

If you order by mail, add $2.00 to your order for shipping.
Prices are subject to change without notice.